MW01133549

WORD BY WORD BASIC

Second Edition

ENGLISH/ HAITIAN KREYOL

DIKSYONNÈ ANGLE AK PÒTRE

Steven J. Molinsky • Bill Bliss

Edwidge Crevecoeur-Bryant, Translator

Illustrated by
Richard E. Hill

PEARSON
Longman

Word by Word Basic Picture Dictionary, English/Haitian Kreyol second edition

Pearson Education, 10 Bank Street, White Plains, NY 10606

Editorial director: Pam Fishman
Vice president, director of design and production: Rhea Banker
Director of electronic production: Aliza Greenblatt
Director of manufacturing: Patrice Fraccio
Senior manufacturing manager: Edith Pullman
Director of marketing: Oliva Fernandez
Associate development editor: Mary Perrotta Rich
Senior digital layout specialist: Wendy Wolf
Text design: Wendy Wolf
Cover design: Tracey Munz Cataldo/Warren Fischbach
Realia creation: Warren Fischbach, Paula Williams
Illustrations: Richard E. Hill
Contributing artists: Steven Young, Charles Cawley, Willard Gage, Marlon Violette
Reviewers: Jean-Claude Borgella, Miami Dade Public Schools, Miami, Florida; Roland Crevecoeur,
Florida School for the Deaf and Blind at St. Augustine
Project management by TransPac Education Services, Victoria, BC, Canada with assistance from
Robert Zacharias & Studio G

Additional photos/illustration: Page **244** *top* U.S. National Archives & Records Administration

ISBN 0-13-148235-1
ISBN 13 9780131482357
Longman on the Web
Longman.com offers online resources for teachers and students. Access our Companion Websites,
our online catalog, and our local offices around the world.

Visit us at longman.com.

Printed in the United States of America
1 2 3 4 5 6 7 8 9 10 – QWD – 12 11 10 09 08 07

Dedicated to Janet Johnston in honor of her wonderful contribution to the development of our textbooks over three decades.

Steven J. Molinsky
Bill Bliss

CONTENTS

SA KI NAN LIV SA A

Unit / Theme	Communication Skills	Writing & Discussion	CASAS	LAUSD	LCPs
1 **Personal Information and Family**	• Asking for & giving personal information • Identifying information on a form • Spelling name aloud • Identifying family members • Introducing others	• Telling about yourself • Telling about family members • Drawing a family tree	0.1.2, 0.1.4, 0.2.1, 0.2.2	*Beg. Literacy:* 1, 2, 3, 4, 5 *Beg. Low:* 1, 2, 4, 6, 7, 9, 58 *Beg. High:* 1, 4, 5, 6	*Literacy LCPs:* 01, 02, 07, 08, 15, 16 *LCP A:* 05, 14, 15 *LCP B:* 22, 31 *LCP C:* 39
2 **At School**	• Identifying classroom objects • Identifying classroom locations • Identifying classroom actions • Giving & following simple classroom commands • Identifying school locations & personnel	• Describing a classroom • Describing a school • Comparing schools in different countries	0.1.2, 0.1.5	*Beg. Literacy:* 8, 9, 11 *Beg. Low:* 12, 13, 15, 16, 17, 18 *Beg. High:* 12, 14, 15	*Literacy LCPs:* 01, 07, 15
3 **Common Everyday Activities and Language**	• Identifying everyday & leisure activities • Inquiring by phone about a person's activities • Asking about a person's plan for future activities • Social communication: Greeting people, Leave taking, Introducing yourself & others, Getting someone's attention, Expressing gratitude, Saying you don't understand, Calling someone on the telephone • Describing the weather • Interpreting temperatures on a thermometer (Fahrenheit & Centigrade) • Describing the weather forecast for tomorrow	• Making a list of daily activities • Describing daily routine • Making a list of planned activities • Describing favorite leisure activities • Describing the weather	0.1.1, 0.1.2, 0.1.4, 0.1.6, 0.2.1, 0.2.4, 1.1.5, 2.1.8, 2.3.3, 7.5.5, 7.5.6, 8.2.3, 8.2.5	*Beg. Literacy:* 5, 6 *Beg. Low:* 9, 11, 12, 13, 28, 29 *Beg. High:* 7a, 7b, 11, 26	*Literacy LCPs:* 01, 02, 07, 08, 15, 16 *LCP A:* 05, 06, 13 *LCP B:* 22, 30 *LCP C:* 39, 47

CASAS: Comprehensive Adult Student Assessment System
LAUSD: Los Angeles Unified School District content standards *(Beginning Literacy, Beginning Low, Beginning High)*
LCPs: Literacy Completion Points – Florida & Texas workforce development skills & life skills –
   (Literacy levels; LCP A – Literacy/Foundations; LCP B – Low Beginning; LCP C – High Beginning)

Unit / Theme	Communication Skills	Writing & Discussion	CASAS	LAUSD	LCPs
4 **Numbers/ Time/ Money/ Calendar**	• Using cardinal & ordinal numbers • Giving information about age, number of family members, residence • Telling time • Indicating time of events • Asking for information about arrival & departure times • Identifying coins & currency – names & values • Making & asking for change • Identifying days of the week • Identifying months of the year • Asking about the year, month, day, date • Asking about the date of a birthday, anniversary, appointment • Giving date of birth	• Describing numbers of students in a class • Identifying a country's population • Describing daily schedule with times • Telling about the use of time in different cultures or countries • Describing the cost of purchases • Describing coins & currency of other countries • Describing weekday activities • Telling about favorite day of the week & month of the year	0.1.2, 0.2.1, 1.1.6, 2.3.1, 2.3.2	*Beg. Literacy:* 6, 12, 13 *Beg. Low:* 3, 4, 25, 26, 30 *Beg. High:* 2, 5	*Literacy LCPs:* 01, 03, 07, 09, 15, 17 *LCP A:* 08 *LCP B:* 25 *LCP C:* 42
5 **Home**	• Identifying types of housing & communities • Requesting a taxi • Calling 911 for an ambulance • Identifying rooms of a home • Identifying furniture • Complimenting • Asking for information in a store • Locating items in a store • Asking about items on sale • Asking the location of items at home • Telling about past weekend activities • Identifying locations in an apartment building • Identifying ways to look for housing: classified ads, listings, vacancy signs • Renting an apartment • Describing household problems • Securing home repair services • Making a suggestion • Identifying household cleaning items • Identifying tools and home supplies • Asking to borrow an item	• Describing types of housing where people live • Describing rooms & furniture in a residence • Telling about baby products & early child-rearing practices in different countries • Telling about personal experiences with repairing things • Describing an apartment building • Describing household cleaning chores	0.1.2, 0.1.4, 1.4.1, 1.4.2, 1.4.7, 2.1.2, 7.5.5, 8.2.5, 8.2.6	*Beg. Low:* 12, 13, 21, 38, 39 *Beg. High:* 10c, 20, 37, 38, 39	*Literacy LCPs:* 01, 07, 11, 15, 19 *LCP A:* 04, 06, 11 *LCP B:* 21 *LCP C:* 38, 40, 45
6 **Community**	• Identifying places in the community • Exchanging greetings • Asking & giving the location of places in the community • Identifying government buildings, services, & other places in a city/town center • Identifying modes of transportation in a city/town center	• Describing places in a neighborhood • Making a list of places, people, & actions observed at an intersection	0.1.2, 0.1.4, 2.5.3, 2.5.4	*Beg. Literacy:* 5, 11 *Beg. Low:* 22, 23, 24 *Beg. High:* 23	*Literacy LCPs:* 01, 04, 07, 11, 15 *LCP A:* 05, 12 *LCP B:* 29 *LCP C:* 46

Unit / Theme	Communication Skills	Writing & Discussion	CASAS	LAUSD	LCPs
7 **Describing**	• Describing people by age • Describing people by physical characteristics • Describing a suspect or missing person to a police officer • Describing people & things using adjectives • Describing physical states & emotions • Expressing concern about another person's physical state or emotion	• Describing physical characteristics of yourself & family members • Describing physical characteristics of a favorite actor or actress or other famous person • Describing things at home & in the community • Telling about personal experiences with different emotions	0.1.2, 0.2.1	Beg. Literacy: 7 Beg. Low: 6 Beg. High: 3, 7b	Literacy LCPs: 01, 07, 15 LCP A: 05 LCP B: 22 LCP C: 39, 49
8 **Food**	• Identifying food items (fruits, vegetables, meat, poultry, seafood, dairy products, juices, beverages, deli, frozen foods, snack foods, groceries) • Identifying non-food items purchased in a supermarket (e.g., household supplies, baby products, pet food) • Determining food needs to make a shopping list • Asking the location of items in a supermarket • Identifying supermarket sections • Requesting items at a service counter in a supermarket • Identifying supermarket checkout area personnel & items • Identifying food containers & quantities • Identifying units of measure • Asking for & giving recipe instructions • Complimenting someone on a recipe • Offering to help with food preparation • Identifying food preparation actions • Ordering fast food items, coffee shop items, & sandwiches • Indicating a shortage of supplies to a co-worker or supervisor • Taking customers' orders at a food service counter • Identifying restaurant objects, personnel, & actions • Making & following requests at work • Identifying & correctly positioning silverware & plates in a table setting • Inquiring in person about restaurant job openings • Ordering from a restaurant menu • Taking customers' orders as a waiter or waitress in a restaurant	• Describing favorite & least favorite foods • Describing foods in different countries • Making a shopping list • Describing places to shop for food • Telling about differences between supermarkets & food stores in different countries • Making a list of items in kitchen cabinets & the refrigerator • Describing recycling practices • Describing a favorite recipe using units of measure • Telling about experience with different types of restaurants • Describing restaurants and menus in different countries • Describing favorite foods ordered in restaurants	0.1.2, 0.1.4, 1.1.1, 1.1.7, 1.3.7, 1.3.8, 2.6.4, 4.8.3	Beg. Literacy: 5, 14 Beg. Low: 14, 32, 35, 37 Beg. High: 10c, 30, 31, 34, 36	Literacy LCPs: 01, 05, 07, 12, 15, 20 LCP A: 05, 07, 11 LCP B: 24, 28 LCP C: 45

Unit / Theme	Communication Skills	Writing & Discussion	CASAS	LAUSD	LCPs
9 **Colors, Clothing, & Shopping**	• Identifying colors • Complimenting someone on clothing • Identifying clothing items, including outerwear, sleepwear, underwear, exercise clothing, footwear, jewelry, & accessories • Talking about appropriate clothing for different weather conditions • Expressing clothing needs to a store salesperson • Locating clothing items • Inquiring about ownership of found clothing items • Indicating loss of a clothing item • Asking about sale prices in a clothing store • Reporting theft of a clothing item to the police • Stating preferences during clothing shopping • Expressing problems with clothing & the need for alterations • Identifying departments & services in a department store • Asking the location of items in a department store • Asking to buy, return, exchange, try on, & pay for department store items • Asking about regular & sales prices, discounts, & sales tax • Interpreting a sales receipt • Offering assistance to customers as a salesperson • Expressing needs to a salesperson in a store • Identifying electronics products, including video & audio equipment, telephones, cameras, & computers • Identifying components of a computer & common computer software • Complimenting someone about an item & inquiring where it was purchased	• Describing the flags of different countries • Telling about emotions associated with different colors • Telling about clothing & colors you like to wear • Describing clothing worn at different occasions (e.g., going to schools, parties, weddings) • Telling about clothing worn in different weather conditions • Telling about clothing worn during exercise activities • Telling about footwear worn during different activities • Describing the color, size, & pattern of favorite clothing items • Comparing clothing fashions now & a long time ago • Describing a department store • Telling about stores that have sales • Telling about an item purchased on sale • Comparing different types & brands of video & audio equipment, telephones, & cameras • Describing personal use of a computer • Sharing opinions about why computers are important	0.1.2, 0.1.3, 0.1.4, 1.1.9, 1.2.1, 1.2.2, 1.2.3, 1.3.3, 1.3.7, 1.3.9, 1.6.3, 1.6.4, 4.8.3, 8.2.4	*Beg. Literacy:* 5, 8, 13, 14 *Beg. Low:* 14, 31, 32, 33, 34 *Beg. High:* 10c, 30, 33, 60	*Literacy LCPs:* 01, 04, 07, 11, 15, 19 *LCP A:* 05, 11, 15 *LCP B:* 28 *LCP C:* 45

Unit / Theme	Communication Skills	Writing & Discussion	CASAS	LAUSD	LCPs
10 **Community Services**	• Requesting bank services & transactions (e.g., deposit, withdrawal, cashing a check, obtaining traveler's checks, opening an account, applying for a loan, exchanging currency) • Identifying bank personnel • Identifying bank forms • Asking about acceptable forms of payment (cash, check, credit card, money order, traveler's check) • Identifying household bills (rent, utilities, etc.) • Identifying family finance documents & actions • Following instructions to use an ATM machine • Requesting post office services & transactions • Identifying types of mail & mail services • Identifying different ways to buy stamps • Requesting non-mail services available at the post office (money order, selective service registration, passport application) • Identifying & locating library sections, services, & personnel • Asking how to find a book in the library • Identifying community institutions, services, and personnel (police, fire, city government, public works, recreation, sanitation, religious institutions) • Identifying types of emergency vehicles	• Describing use of bank services • Telling about household bills & amounts paid • Telling about the person responsible for household finances • Describing use of ATM machines • Describing use of postal services • Comparing postal systems in different countries • Telling about experience using a library • Telling about the location of community institutions • Describing experiences using community institutions	0.1.2, 1.3.1, 1.3.3, 1.4.4, 1.5.1, 1.5.3, 1.8.1, 1.8.2, 1.8.4, 2.4.1, 2.4.2, 2.4.4, 2.5.1, 2.5.4, 2.5.6, 8.2.1	*Beg. Low:* 8 *Beg. High:* 24, 28, 29	*Literacy LCPs:* 01, 07, 15, 19 *LCP A:* 08, 11, 12 *LCP B:* 25, 28, 29 *LCP C:* 42, 44, 46

Unit / Theme	Communication Skills	Writing & Discussion	CASAS	LAUSD	LCPs
11 Health	• Identifying parts of the body & key internal organs • Describing ailments, symptoms, & injuries • Asking about the health of another person • Identifying items in a first-aid kit • Describing medical emergencies • Identifying emergency medical procedures (CPR, rescue breathing, Heimlich maneuver) • Calling 911 to report a medical emergency • Identifying major illnesses • Talking with a friend or co-worker about illness in one's family • Following instructions during a medical examination • Identifying medical personnel, equipment, & supplies in medical & dental offices • Understanding medical & dental personnel's description of procedures during treatment • Understanding a doctor's medical advice and instructions • Identifying over-the-counter medications • Understanding dosage instructions on medicine labels • Identifying hospital departments & personnel • Identifying equipment in a hospital room • Identifying actions & items related to personal hygiene • Locating personal care products in a store • Identifying actions & items related to baby care	• Describing self • Telling about a personal experience with an illness or injury • Describing remedies or treatments for common problems (cold, stomachache, insect bite, hiccups) • Describing experience with a medical emergency • Describing a medical examination • Describing experience with a medical or dental procedure • Telling about medical advice received • Telling about over-the-counter medications used • Comparing use of medications in different countries • Describing a hospital stay • Making a list of personal care items needed for a trip • Comparing baby products in different countries	0.1.2, 0.1.4, 1.3.7, 2.1.2, 2.5.3, 2.5.9, 3.1.1, 3.1.2, 3.1.3, 3.3.1, 3.3.2, 3.3.3, 3.4.2, 3.4.3, 3.5.4, 3.5.5, 3.5.9, 8.1.1	*Beg. Literacy:* 9 *Beg. Low:* 12, 21, 32, 43, 44, 45, 46 *Beg. High:* 10b, 20, 30, 43, 45, 46, 47, 50	*Literacy LCPs:* 01, 05, 06, 07, 12, 14, 15, 20, 22 *LCP A:* 06, 07, 10, 14 *LCP B:* 24, 27 *LCP C:* 40, 41, 44, 48

Unit / Theme	Communication Skills	Writing & Discussion	CASAS	LAUSD	LCPs

12 **School Subjects and Activities**	• Identifying school subjects
	• Identifying extracurricular activities
	• Sharing after-school plans
	• MATH:
	  • Asking & answering basic questions during a math class
	  • Using fractions to indicate sale prices
	  • Using percents to indicate test scores & probability in weather forecasts
	  • Identifying high school math subjects
	  • Using measurement terms to indicate height, width, depth, length, distance
	  • Interpreting metric measurements
	  • Identifying types of lines, geometric shapes, & solid figures
	• ENGLISH LANGUAGE ARTS:
	  • Identifying types of sentences
	  • Identifying parts of speech
	  • Identifying punctuation marks
	  • Providing feedback during peer-editing
	  • Identifying steps of the writing process
	  • Identifying types of literature
	  • Identifying forms of writing
	• GEOGRAPHY:
	  • Identifying geographical features & bodies of water
	  • Identifying natural environments (desert, jungle, rainforest, etc.)
	• SCIENCE:
	  • Identifying science classroom/laboratory equipment
	  • Asking about equipment needed to do a science procedure
	  • Identifying steps of the scientific method
		• Telling about favorite school subject
		• Telling about extracurricular activities
		• Comparing extracurricular activities in different countries
		• Describing math education
		• Telling about something bought on sale
		• Researching & sharing information about population statistics using percents
		• Describing favorite books & authors
		• Describing newspapers & magazines read
		• Telling about use of different types of written communication
		• Describing the geography of your country
		• Describing geographical features experienced
		• Describing experience with scientific equipment
		• Describing science education
		• Brainstorming a science experiment & describing each step of the scientific method
			0.1.2,
			0.1.3,
			0.1.5,
			0.2.3,
			1.1.2,
			1.1.4,
			2.5.5,
			2.5.9,
			2.7.5,
			5.2.5,
			6.0.1,
			6.0.2,
			6.0.4,
			6.1.1,
			6.1.2,
			6.1.3,
			6.1.4,
			6.4.1,
			6.4.2,
			6.6.1,
			6.6.2,
			6.8.1
				Beg. Literacy: 15
				Beg. Low: 12, 16, 17
				Beg. High: 7a, 14, 31
					Literacy LCPs: 01, 07, 15
					LCP A: 14
					LCP B: 31
					LCP C: 39, 48

Unit / Theme	Communication Skills	Writing & Discussion	CASAS	LAUSD	LCPs
13 **Work**	• Identifying occupations • Talking about occupation during social conversation • Identifying job skills & work activities • Indicating job skills during an interview • Identifying types of job advertisements (help wanted signs, job notices, classified ads) • Interpreting abbreviations in job advertisements • Identifying each step in a job-search process • Making requests at work • Identifying factory locations, equipment, & personnel • Asking the location of workplace departments & personnel to orient oneself as a new employee • Asking about the location & activities of a co-worker • Identifying construction site machinery, equipment, and building materials • Asking a co-worker for a workplace item • Warning a co-worker of a safety hazard • Asking whether there is a sufficient supply of workplace materials • Identifying job safety equipment • Interpreting warning signs at work • Reminding someone to use safety equipment • Asking the location of emergency equipment at work	• Career exploration: sharing ideas about occupations that are interesting, difficult, important • Describing occupation & occupations of family members • Describing job skills • Describing a familiar job (skill requirements, qualifications, hours, salary) • Telling about how people found their jobs • Telling about experience with a job search or job interview • Describing a nearby factory & working conditions there • Comparing products produced by factories in different countries • Describing building materials used in ones dwelling • Describing a nearby construction site • Telling about experience with safety equipment • Describing the use of safety equipment in the community	0.1.2, 0.1.6, 4.1.2, 4.1.3, 4.1.5, 4.1.6, 4.1.7, 4.1.8, 4.3.1, 4.3.3, 4.3.4, 4.5.1, 4.6.1, 7.1.1, 7.5.5	*Beg. Literacy:* 5, 10 *Beg. Low:* 11, 12, 14, 48, 49, 50, 51, 52, 53, 54, 56 *Beg. High:* 7a, 8a, 11, 51, 54	*Literacy LCPs:* 01, 07, 10, 14, 15, 18, 22 *LCP A:* 01, 02, 03, 04, 10 *LCP B:* 18, 19, 20, 21, 27 *LCP C:* 35, 36, 38, 44
14 **Transportation and Travel**	• Identifying modes of local & inter-city public transportation • Expressing intended mode of travel • Asking about a location to obtain transportation (bus stop, bus station, train station, subway station) • Locating ticket counters, information booths, fare card machines, & information signage in transportation stations • Giving & following driving directions (using prepositions of motion) • Interpreting traffic signs • Warning a driver about an upcoming sign • Interpreting compass directions • Asking for driving directions • Following instructions during a driver's test • Repeating to confirm instructions • Identifying airport locations & personnel (check-in, security, gate, baggage claim, Customs & Immigration) • Asking for location of places & personnel at an airport • Indicating loss of travel documents or other items	• Describing mode of travel to different places in the community • Describing local public transportation • Comparing transportation in different countries • Describing your route from home to school • Describing how to get to different places from home and school • Describing local traffic signs • Comparing traffic signs in different countries • Describing a familiar airport • Telling about an experience with Customs & Immigration	0.1.2, 0.1.3, 0.1.6, 1.9.1, 1.9.2, 1.9.4, 2.2.1, 2.2.2, 2.2.3, 2.2.4, 2.5.4	*Beg. Literacy:* 5, 10 *Beg. Low:* 11, 13, 23, 24, 42, 48, 49 *Beg. High:* 11, 23, 41	*Literacy LCPs:* 01, 04, 06, 07, 13, 15, 21 *LCP A:* 09 *LCP B:* 26 *LCP C:* 43

Unit / Theme	Communication Skills	Writing & Discussion	CASAS	LAUSD	LCPs
15 **Recreation and Entertainment**	• Identifying places to go for outdoor recreation, entertainment, culture, etc. • Asking for & offering a suggestion for a leisure activity • Describing past weekend activities • Describing activities planned for a future day off or weekend • Identifying individual sports & recreation activities • Asking and telling about favorite sports and recreation activities • Describing exercise habits & routines • Identifying team sports & terms for players & playing fields • Commenting on a player's performance during a game • Engaging in small talk about favorite sports, teams, and players • Identifying types of entertainment & cultural events • Identifying different genres of music, movies, & TV programs • Expressing likes about types of entertainment	• Describing favorite places to go & activities there • Describing favorite individual sports & recreation activities • Comparing individual sports & recreation activities popular in different countries • Describing favorite team sports & famous players • Telling about favorite types of entertainment • Comparing types of entertainment popular in different countries • Telling about favorite performers • Telling about favorite types of music, movies, & TV programs	0.1.2, 0.1.3, 0.1.4, 0.2.4, 2.6.1, 2.6.2, 2.6.3, 2.7.6, 3.5.8, 3.5.9	*Beg. Low:* 12, 13, 14 *Beg. High:* 7a	*Literacy LCPs:* 01, 07, 15 *LCP A:* 05, 06 *LCP C:* 39
16 **U.S. Civics**	• Producing correct form of identification when requested (driver's license, social security card, student I.D. card, employee I.D. badge, permanent resident card, passport, visa, work permit, birth certificate, proof of residence) • Identifying the three branches of U.S. government (legislative, executive, judicial) & their functions • Identifying senators, representatives, the president, vice-president, cabinet, Supreme Court justices, & the chief justice, & the branches of government in which they work • Identifying the key buildings in each branch of government (Capitol Building, White House, Supreme Court Building) • Identifying the Constitution as "the supreme law of the land" • Identifying the Bill of Rights • Naming freedoms guaranteed by the 1st Amendment • Identifying key amendments to the Constitution • Identifying key holidays & dates they occur	• Telling about forms of identification & when needed • Comparing the governments of different countries • Describing how people in a community "exercise their 1st Amendment rights" • Brainstorming ideas for a new amendment to the Constitution • Describing U.S. holidays you celebrate • Describing holidays celebrated in different countries	0.1.2, 0.1.3, 2.7.1, 5.1.6, 5.2.1, 5.2.2, 5.5.2, 5.5.3, 5.5.4	*Beg. Low:* 40 *Beg. High:* 40, 42	*Literacy LCPs:* 01, 07, 15 *LCP A:* 12 *LCP B:* 26, 29 *LCP C:* 43, 46

Welcome to the second edition of the WORD BY WORD BASIC Picture Dictionary! This text presents more than 2,500 vocabulary words through vibrant illustrations and simple accessible lesson pages with large type that are designed for clarity and ease-of-use with learners at low-beginning and literacy levels. Our goal is to prepare students for success using English in everyday life, in the community, in school, and at work.

WORD BY WORD BASIC is an abridged version of the "full" *Word by Word* Picture Dictionary. It organizes the vocabulary into 16 thematic units, providing a careful research-based sequence of lessons that integrates students' development of grammar and vocabulary skills through topics that begin with the immediate world of the student and progress to the world at large. Early lessons on the family, the home, and daily activities lead to lessons on the community, school, workplace, shopping, recreation, and other topics. The text offers extensive coverage of important lifeskill competencies and the vocabulary of school subjects and extracurricular activities, and it is designed to meet the objectives of current national, state, and local standards-based curricula you can find in the Scope & Sequence on the previous pages.

Since each lesson in *Word by Word Basic* is self-contained, it can be used either sequentially or in any desired order. For users' convenience, the lessons are listed in two ways: sequentially in the Table of Contents, and alphabetically in the Thematic Index. These resources, combined with the Glossary in the appendix, allow students and teachers to quickly and easily locate all words and topics in the Picture Dictionary.

The *Word by Word Basic* Picture Dictionary is the centerpiece of the complete *Word by Word Basic* Vocabulary Development Program, which offers a wide selection of print and media support materials for instruction at all levels.

A unique choice of workbooks offers flexible options to meet students' needs. A Vocabulary Workbook features motivating vocabulary, grammar, and listening practice. A standards-based Lifeskills Workbook provides competency-based activities and reading tied to national, state, and local curriculum frameworks. A Literacy Workbook offers fundamental practice with the alphabet and basic reading and writing skills for pre-Beginners.

The Teacher's Guide and Lesson Planner with CD-ROM includes lesson-planning suggestions, community tasks, Internet weblinks, and reproducible masters to save teachers hours of lesson preparation time. A Handbook of Vocabulary Teaching Strategies is included in the Teacher's Guide. The CD-ROM contains a complete Activity Bank of reproducible grammar and vocabulary worksheets for each unit and innovative level-specific lesson-planning forms that teachers can fill in and print out for quick and easy lesson preparation.

The Audio Program includes all words and conversations for interactive practice and—as bonus material—an expanded selection of WordSongs for entertaining musical practice with the vocabulary.

Additional ancillary materials include Color Transparencies, Vocabulary Game Cards, a Testing Program, and ExamView CD-ROM. Bilingual Editions are also available.

Teaching Strategies

Word by Word Basic presents vocabulary words in context. Model conversations depict situations in which people use the words in meaningful communication. These models become the basis for students to engage in dynamic, interactive practice. In addition, writing and discussion questions in each lesson encourage students to relate the vocabulary and themes to their own lives as they share experiences, thoughts, opinions, and information about themselves, their cultures, and their countries. In this way, students get to know each other "word by word."

In using *Word by Word Basic*, we encourage you to develop approaches and strategies that are compatible with your own teaching style and the needs and abilities of your students. You may find it helpful to incorporate some of the following techniques for presenting and practicing the vocabulary in each lesson.

1. **Preview the Vocabulary:** Activate students' prior knowledge of the vocabulary by brainstorming with students the words in the lesson they already know and writing them on the board, or by having students look at the transparency or the illustration in *Word by Word Basic* and identify the words they are familiar with.

2. **Present the Vocabulary:** Using the transparency or the illustration in the Picture Dictionary, point to the picture of each word, say the word, and have the class repeat it chorally and individually. (You can also play the word list on the Audio Program.) Check students' understanding and pronunciation of the vocabulary.

3. **Vocabulary Practice:** Have students practice the vocabulary as a class, in pairs, or in small groups. Say or write a word, and have students point to the item or tell the number. Or, point to an item or give the number, and have students say the word.

4. **Model Conversation Practice:** Some lessons have model conversations that use the first word in the vocabulary list. Other models are in the form of skeletal dialogs, in which vocabulary words can be inserted. (In many skeletal dialogs, bracketed numbers indicate which words can be used for practicing the conversation. If no bracketed numbers appear, all the words in the lesson can be used.)

The following steps are recommended for Model Conversation Practice:

a. Preview: Have students look at the model illustration and discuss who they think the speakers are and where the conversation takes place.

b. The teacher presents the model or plays the audio one or more times and checks students' understanding of the situation and the vocabulary.

c. Students repeat each line of the conversation chorally and individually.

d. Students practice the model in pairs.

e. A pair of students presents a conversation based on the model, but using a different word from the vocabulary list.

f. In pairs, students practice several conversations based on the model, using different words on the page.

g. Pairs present their conversations to the class.

5. **Additional Conversation Practice:** Many lessons provide two additional skeletal dialogs for further conversation practice with the vocabulary. (These can be found in the yellow-shaded area at the bottom of the page.) Have students practice and present these conversations using any words they wish. Before they practice the additional conversations, you may want to have students listen to the sample additional conversations on the Audio Program.

6. **Spelling Practice:** Have students practice spelling the words as a class, in pairs, or in small groups. Say a word, and have students spell it aloud or write it. Or, using the transparency, point to an item and have students write the word.

7. **Themes for Discussion, Composition, Journals, and Portfolios:** Each lesson of *Word by Word Basic* provides one or more questions for discussion and composition. (These can be found in a blue-shaded area at the bottom of the page.) Have students respond to the questions as a class, in pairs, or in small groups. Or, have students write their responses at home, share their written work with other students, and discuss as a class, in pairs, or in small groups. As an alternative for students at literacy and pre-beginning levels, you can use a language experience approach by having students say their responses while you or a teaching assistant or a volunteer writes them down. Students can then practice decoding what they have "written" and then read their responses aloud to another student.

Students may enjoy keeping a journal of their written work. If time permits, you may want to write a response in each student's journal, sharing your own opinions and experiences as well as reacting to what the student has written. If you are keeping portfolios of students' work, these compositions serve as excellent examples of students' progress in learning English.

8. **Communication Activities:** The *Word by Word Basic* Teacher's Guide and Lesson Planner with CD-ROM provides a wealth of games, tasks, brainstorming, discussion, movement, drawing, miming, role-playing, and other activities designed to take advantage of students' different learning styles and particular abilities and strengths. For each lesson, choose one or more of these activities to reinforce students' vocabulary learning in a way that is stimulating, creative, and enjoyable.

WORD BY WORD BASIC aims to offer students a communicative, meaningful, and lively way of practicing English vocabulary. In conveying to you the substance of our program, we hope that we have also conveyed the spirit: that learning vocabulary can be genuinely interactive . . . relevant to our students' lives . . . responsive to students' differing strengths and learning styles . . . and fun!

Steven J. Molinsky
Bill Bliss

ENFÒMASYON PÈSONNÈL

Registration Form

Name _____ Gloria _____ P. _____ Sanchez _____
First _____ Middle Initial _____ Last

Address _____ 95 _____ Garden Street _____ 3G _____
Number _____ Street _____ Apartment Number
_____ Los Angeles _____ CA _____ 90036 _____
City _____ State _____ Zip Code

Telephone __323-524-3278__   Cell Phone __323-695-1864__

E-Mail Address _gloria97@ail.com_   SSN _227-93-6185_   Sex M__ F X

Date of Birth __5/12/88__   Place of Birth __Centerville, Texas__

non	**1**	name	eta	**10**	state
premye non	**2**	first name	kòd postal	**11**	zip code
dezyèm non	**3**	middle initial	areyakòd	**12**	area code
dènye non/siyati/ tinon gate	**4**	last name / family name	nimewo telefòn	**13**	telephone number / phone number
adrès/kote ou rete	**5**	address	nimewo selilè	**14**	cell phone number
nimewo apatman/ nimewo kay	**6**	street number	adrès emèl	**15**	e-mail address
			nimewo sosyal	**16**	social security number
ri/lari	**7**	street	sèks	**17**	sex
nimewo apatman	**8**	apartment number	dat ou fèt	**18**	date of birth
			kote ou fèt	**19**	place of birth
vil/lavil	**9**	city			

A. What's your **name**?
B. Gloria P. Sanchez.

A. What's your _____?
B. ....
A. Did you say ....?
B. Yes. That's right.

A. What's your last name?
B. ....
A. How do you spell that?
B. ....

Tell about yourself:
    My name is ....
    My address is ....
    My telephone number is ....

Now interview a friend:
    What's your name?
    What's your address?
    What's your telephone number?

FAMILY MEMBERS I

MOUN KI NAN LAFANMI I

mari	**1** husband		frè ak sè	**siblings**
madanm	**2** wife		sè	**8** sister
			frè	**9** brother
paran yo	**parents**			
papa	**3** father		**gran paran yo**	**grandparents**
manman	**4** mother		grann	**10** grandmother
			granpapa	**11** grandfather
timoun yo	**children**			
pitit fi	**5** daughter		**pitit-pitit yo**	**grandchildren**
pitit gason	**6** son		pitit-pitit fi	**12** granddaughter
bebe	**7** baby		pitit-pitit gason	**13** grandson

A. Who is he?
B. He's my **husband**.
A. What's his name?
B. His name is *Jack*.

A. Who is she?
B. She's my **wife**.
A. What's her name?
B. Her name is *Nancy*.

A. I'd like to introduce my _____.
B. Nice to meet you.
C. Nice to meet you, too.

A. What's your _____'s name?
B. His/Her name is ....

Who are the people in your family?
What are their names?

Tell about photos of family members.

MOUN KI NAN LAFANMI II

Helen

Walter

Jack

Nancy

Frank

Linda

Jennifer

Timmy

Alan

tonton/	**1** uncle	kouzen/	**5** cousin	bèlfi	**9** daughter-in-law
monnonk		kouzin		bòfrè	**10** brother-in-law
tant/matant	**2** aunt	bèlmè	**6** mother-in-law	bèlsè	**11** sister-in-law
nyès	**3** niece	bòpè	**7** father-in-law		
neve	**4** nephew	bofis	**8** son-in-law		

① Jack is Alan's ___.

② Nancy is Alan's ___.

③ Jennifer is Frank and Linda's ___.

④ Timmy is Frank and Linda's ___.

⑤ Alan is Jennifer and Timmy's ___.

⑥ Helen is Jack's ___.

⑦ Walter is Jack's ___.

⑧ Jack is Helen and Walter's ___.

⑨ Linda is Helen and Walter's ___.

⑩ Frank is Jack's ___.

⑪ Linda is Jack's ___.

A. Who is he/she?

B. He's/She's my _____.

A. What's his/her name?

B. His/Her name is _____.

A. Let me introduce my _____.

B. I'm glad to meet you.

C. Nice meeting you, too.

Tell about your relatives:
  What are their names?
  Where do they live?

Draw your family tree and tell about it.

CLASSROOM OBJECTS

OBJÈ NAN SALKLAS LA

plim	**1** pen	règ	**11** ruler
kreyon	**2** pencil	kalkilatè	**12** calculator
gòm	**3** eraser	lakrè	**13** chalk
tay kreyon/egize	**4** pencil sharpener	chifon	**14** eraser
liv lekòl	**5** book/textbook	makè	**15** marker
liv egzèsis	**6** workbook	klou pinèz	**16** thumbtack
kaye nòt	**7** spiral notebook	klavye	**17** keyboard
klasè	**8** binder/notebook	monitè	**18** monitor
papye delin	**9** notebook paper	sourit	**19** mouse
papye kawo	**10** graph paper	enprimant	**20** printer

[1, 2, 4–13, 15–20]
A. What do you call this in English?
B. It's a **pen**.

A. Where's the _____?
B. Over there.

[1–3, 5–12]
A. Is this your _____?
B. Yes, it is.

[3, 14]
A. What do you call this in English?
B. It's an **eraser**.

Point to objects and people in your classroom and say the words.

SALKLAS LA

pwofesè	**1** teacher	kat jewografi	**12** map
èd pwofesè	**2** teacher's aide	tablo pou afich	**13** bulletin board
elèv	**3** student	wopalè	**14** P.A. system/ loudspeaker
biwo	**4** desk		
chèz	**5** seat/chair	tablo blan	**15** whiteboard
tab	**6** table	glòb lemonn/ glòb tèrès	**16** globe
konpitè	**7** computer		
pwojektè fim transparan	**8** overhead projector	etajè liv	**17** bookcase/ bookshelf
ekran	**9** screen	biwo pwofesè	**18** teacher's desk
tablo	**10** board/ chalkboard		
pandil	**11** clock	kòbèy papye	**19** wastebasket

Practice these conversations with the words on pages 8–11.

A. Where's the **teacher**?
B. The **teacher** is *next to* the **board**.

A. Where's the **globe**?
B. The **globe** is *on* the **bookcase**.

A. Is there a/an ____ in your classroom?*
B. Yes. There's a/an ____ next to/on the ____.

A. Is there a/an ____ in your classroom?*
B. No, there isn't.

Describe your classroom. (There's a/an ....)

* *With 9, 10, 13 on page 9 use:* Is there ____ in your classroom?

AKTIVITE NAN KLAS I

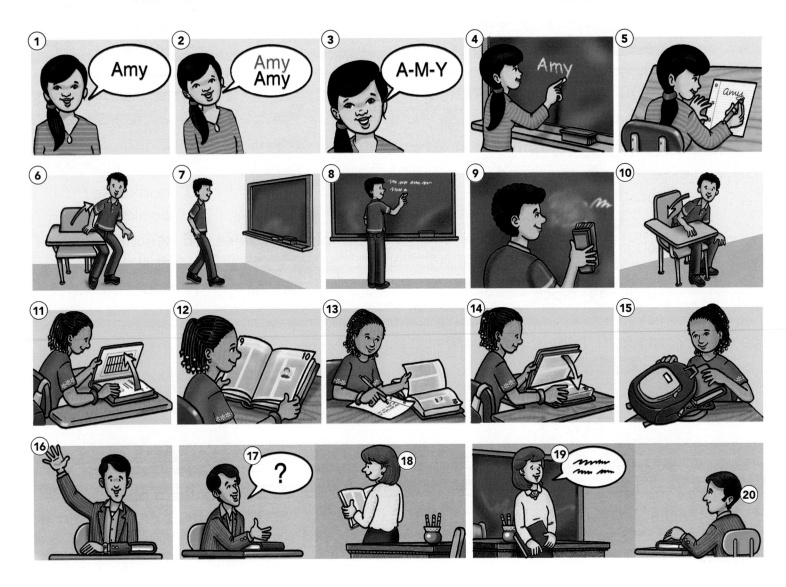

Di non ou.	**1**	Say your name.	Louvri liv ou.	**11** Open your book.
Repete non ou.	**2**	Repeat your name.	Li paj dis.	**12** Read page ten.
Eple non ou.	**3**	Spell your name.	Etidye paj dis.	**13** Study page ten.
Ekri non ou detache.	**4**	Print your name.	Fèmen liv ou.	**14** Close your book.
Siyen non ou.	**5**	Sign your name.	Ranmase liv ou.	**15** Put away your book.

Kanpe.	**6**	Stand up.	Leve men ou.	**16** Raise your hand.
Ale sou tablo a.	**7**	Go to the board.	Mande yon kesyon.	**17** Ask a question.
Ekri sou tablo a.	**8**	Write on the board.	Koute kesyon an.	**18** Listen to the question.
Efase tablo a.	**9**	Erase the board.	Reponn kesyon an.	**19** Answer the question.
Chita/Pran plas ou.	**10**	Sit down. / Take your seat.	Koute repons lan.	**20** Listen to the answer.

You're the teacher.
Give instructions to your students.

AKTIVITE NAN KLAS II

Fè devwa ou.	**1** Do your homework.	Chèche nan diksyonè a.	**11** Look in the dictionary.
Pote devwa ou.	**2** Bring in your homework.	Chèche yon mo.	**12** Look up a word.
Repase repons yo.	**3** Go over the answers.	Pwonnonse mo a.	**13** Pronounce the word.
Korije fòt ou yo.	**4** Correct your mistakes.	Li definisyon an.	**14** Read the definition.
Remèt devwa ou.	**5** Hand in your homework.	Kopye mo a.	**15** Copy the word.

Pataje liv la.	**6** Share a book.	Travay poukont ou.	**16** Work alone./ Do your own work.
Diskite kesyon an.	**7** Discuss the question.	Travay ak yonlòt/ asosye.	**17** Work with a partner.
Youn ede lòt.	**8** Help each other.	Separe an ti gwoup.	**18** Break up into small groups.
Travay ansanm.	**9** Work together.	Travay an gwoup.	**19** Work in a group.
Pataje ak klas la.	**10** Share with the class.	Travay ansanm.	**20** Work as a class.

You're the teacher.
Give instructions to your students.

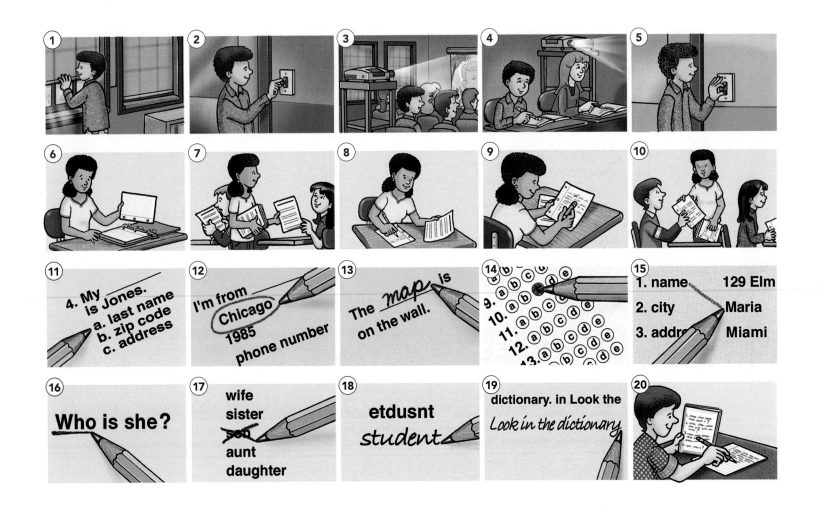

Desann rido yo.	**1**	Lower the shades.
Etenn limyè yo.	**2**	Turn off the lights.
Gade ekran.	**3**	Look at the screen.
Pran nòt.	**4**	Take notes.
Limen limyè yo.	**5**	Turn on the lights.

Chwazi repons ki pi bon an.	**11**	Choose the correct answer.
Mete yon wonn nan repons ki pi bon an.	**12**	Circle the correct answer.
Ekri nan espas vid la.	**13**	Fill in the blank.
Make repons lan sou papye.	**14**	Mark the answer sheet. / Bubble the answer.
Konekte mo yo.	**15**	Match the words.

Retire yon fèy papye.	**6**	Take out a piece of paper.
Pase fèy egzamen yo.	**7**	Pass out the tests.
Reponn kesyon yo.	**8**	Answer the questions.
Tcheke repons yo.	**9**	Check your answers.
Ranmase egzamen yo.	**10**	Collect the tests.

Pase yon trè anba mo a.	**16**	Underline the word.
Pase yon kwa sou mo a.	**17**	Cross out the word.
Demelanje mo yo.	**18**	Unscramble the word.
Mete mo yo annòd.	**19**	Put the words in order.
Ekri nan yon lòt papye.	**20**	Write on a separate sheet of paper.

You're the teacher.
Give instructions to your students.

PREPOSITIONS

PREPOZISYON

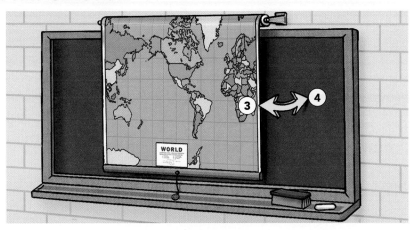

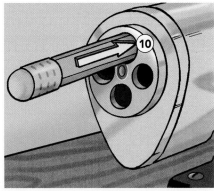

anlè	**1** above		agòch	**8** to the left of
anba	**2** below		adwat	**9** to the right of
devan	**3** in front of		anndan	**10** in
dèyè	**4** behind		nan mitan	**11** between
sou kote	**5** next to			
sou	**6** on			
anba	**7** under			

[1–10]
A. Where's the *clock*?
B. The *clock* is **above** the *bulletin board*.

[11]
A. Where's the *dictionary*?
B. The *dictionary* is **between** the *globe* and the *pencil sharpener*.

Tell about the classroom on page 10. Use the prepositions in this lesson.

Tell about your classroom.

PEOPLE AND PLACES AT SCHOOL

MOUN AK KOTE NAN LEKÒL

biwo	**A** office		sekretè lekòl	**1** clerk / (school) secretary
biwo direktè	**B** principal's office		direktè	**2** principal
enfimri/biwo enfimyè	**C** nurse's office		enfimyè	**3** school nurse
biwo konseye	**D** guidance office		konseye gid	**4** guidance counselor
saldeklas	**E** classroom		pwofesè	**5** teacher
koridò	**F** hallway		asistan direktè	**6** assistant principal / vice-principal
kazye elèv	**a** locker			
laboratwa syans	**G** science lab		ofisye sekirite	**7** security officer
jimnazyòm	**H** gym		pwofesè syans	**8** science teacher
sal kazye elèv	**a** locker room		pwofesè edikasyon fizik	**9** P.E. teacher
teren kous	**I** track		antrenè	**10** coach
estrad	**a** bleachers		jeran	**11** custodian
teren espò	**J** field		anplwaye kafeterya	**12** cafeteria worker
oditoryòm	**K** auditorium		siveyan kafeterya	**13** lunchroom monitor
kafeterya	**L** cafeteria		bibliyotèk lekòl	**14** school librarian
bibliyotèk	**M** library			

A. Where are you going?
B. I'm going to the ___[A–D, G–M]___ .
A. Do you have a hall pass?
B. Yes. Here it is.

A. Where's the ___[1–14]___ ?
B. He's / She's } in the ___[A–M]___ .

Describe the school where you study English.
Tell about the rooms, offices, and people.

Tell about differences between the school in
this lesson and schools in your country.

EVERYDAY ACTIVITIES I

AKTIVITE TOULEJOU I

leve	**1**	get up	dezabiye	**11**	get undressed
pran yon douch	**2**	take a shower	benyen	**12**	take a bath
bwose dan *mwen*	**3**	brush *my** teeth	ale kouche	**13**	go to bed
fè labab	**4**	shave	dòmi	**14**	sleep
abiye	**5**	get dressed	fè manje maten	**15**	make breakfast
lave figi *mwen*	**6**	wash *my** face	fè manje midi/lench	**16**	make lunch
makiye	**7**	put on makeup	fè manje aswè	**17**	cook/make dinner
bwose tèt *mwen*	**8**	brush *my** hair	manje manje maten	**18**	eat/have breakfast
penyen tèt *mwen*	**9**	comb *my** hair	manje manje midi/ lench	**19**	eat/have lunch
fè kabann nan	**10**	make the bed	manje aswè	**20**	eat/have dinner

* my, his, her, our, your, their

A. What do you do every day?
B. I **get up**, I **take a shower**, and I **brush my teeth**.

A. What does he do every day?
B. He _____s, he _____s, and he _____s.

A. What does she do every day?
B. She _____s, she _____s, and she_____s.

What do you do every day? Make a list.

Interview some friends and tell about their everyday activities.

netwaye apatman an/	**1**	clean the apartment/	al nan travay	**9**	go to work
netwaye kay la		clean the house	al lekòl	**10**	go to school
lave vesèl la	**2**	wash the dishes	kondui al travay	**11**	drive to work
fè lesiv	**3**	do the laundry	pran bis pou ale lekòl	**12**	take the bus to school
pase fè	**4**	iron			
bay bebe a manje	**5**	feed the baby	travay	**13**	work
bay chat la manje	**6**	feed the cat	kite travay	**14**	leave work
pwonmennen chen an	**7**	walk the dog	al nan makèt	**15**	go to the store
etidye	**8**	study	vin lakay	**16**	come home

A. Hello. What are you doing?
B. I'm **clean**ing the **apartment**.

A. Hello, ... This is ....
What are you doing?
B. I'm _____ing. How about you?
A. I'm _____ing.

A. Are you going to _____ soon?
B. Yes. I'm going to _____ in a little while.

What are you going to do tomorrow? Make a list of everything you are going to do.

LEISURE ACTIVITIES

AKTIVITE LIB

gade televizyon	**1** watch TV		jwe gita	**9** play the guitar
koute radyo	**2** listen to the radio		pratike pyano	**10** practice the piano
tande mizik	**3** listen to music		egzèsis	**11** exercise
li yon liv	**4** read a book		naje	**12** swim
li jounal	**5** read the newspaper		plante flè	**13** plant flowers
			sèvi ak òdinatè	**14** use the computer
jwe	**6** play		ekri yon lèt	**15** write a letter
jwe kat	**7** play cards		repoze	**16** relax
jwe baskèt	**8** play basketball			

A. Hi. What are you doing?
B. I'm **watch**ing **TV**.

A. Hi, ... Are you
   _____ing?
B. No, I'm not. I'm _____ing.

A. What's your (husband/wife/son/
   daughter/. . .) doing?
B. He's/She's _____ing.

What leisure activities do you like to do?

What do your family members and friends like to do?

EVERYDAY CONVERSATION I

KONVÈSASYON TOULEJOU I

Greeting People

Ap Salye Moun

Leave Taking

Ap Di Orevwa

Alo.	**1**	Hello. / Hi.
Bonjou.	**2**	Good morning.
Bòn apremidi.	**3**	Good afternoon.
Bonswa.	**4**	Good evening.
Kouman ou ye?	**5**	How are you? / How are you doing?
Byen./Byen mèsi./Pa mal.	**6**	Fine. / Fine, thanks. / Okay.
Sak nouvo kounye a?/	**7**	What's new?/
Sak nouvo avè w kounye a?		What's new with you?
Pa anpil./Pa twò anpil.	**8**	Not much. / Not too much.
Orevwa.	**9**	Good-bye. / Bye.
Bònnwit.	**10**	Good night.
Na wè pi ta./Na wè toutalè.	**11**	See you later. / See you soon.

Practice conversations with other students.
Use all the expressions in this lesson.

Introducing Yourself and Others
Ap Prezante Ou Ba Lòt

Getting Someone's Attention
Ap Atire Atansyon Yon Moun

Expressing Gratitude
Ap Montre Rekonesans

Saying You Don't Understand
Ap Di Ou Pa Konprann

Calling Someone on the Telephone
Ap Rele Yon Moun nan Telefòn

Alo. Mwen rele ..../Alo. M rele	**1**	Hello. My name is ..../Hi. I'm ....
Mwen kontan fè konesans ou.	**2**	Nice to meet you.
Mwen kontan fè konesans ou tou.	**3**	Nice to meet you, too.
M ta renmen prezante ..../Se	**4**	I'd like to introduce ..../This is ....
Eskize m.	**5**	Excuse me.
Èske mwen ka poze yon kesyon?	**6**	May I ask a question?
Mèsi.	**7**	Thank you./Thanks.
Padkwa.	**8**	You're welcome.
Mwen pa konprann./ Eskize m. Mwen pa konprann.	**9**	I don't understand./ Sorry. I don't understand.
Èske ou ka repete l ankò?/ Èske ou ka dil ankò?	**10**	Can you please repeat that?/ Can you please say that again?
Alo. Se .... Èske m ka pale ak ......?	**11**	Hello. This is .... May I please speak to ......?
Wi. Tann yon segonn.	**12**	Yes. Hold on a moment.
Eskize m. .... a la kounye a.	**13**	I'm sorry. .... isn't here right now.

Practice conversations with other students.
Use all the expressions in this lesson.

THE WEATHER

TAN

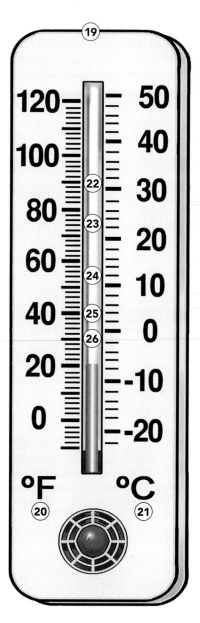

Tan		Weather
bèl solèy	**1**	sunny
nyaj kouvri	**2**	cloudy
fè klè	**3**	clear
tan sonm	**4**	hazy
gen bwouya	**5**	foggy
lafimen ak pousyè	**6**	smoggy
lap vante	**7**	windy
fè imid	**8**	humid / muggy
gen lapli	**9**	raining
lapli ap farinen	**10**	drizzling
gen nèj	**11**	snowing
gen grèl	**12**	hailing
lagrèl ap tonbe	**13**	sleeting
zèklè	**14**	lightning

loraj	**15**	thunderstorm
tanpèt nèj	**16**	snowstorm
tanpèt pousyè	**17**	dust storm
vag chalè	**18**	heat wave

Tanperatii		Temperature
tèmomèt	**19**	thermometer
Farennayt	**20**	Fahrenheit
Santigrad	**21**	Centigrade / Celsius
cho	**22**	hot
tyèd	**23**	warm
fre	**24**	cool
frèt	**25**	cold
glase	**26**	freezing

[1–13]

A. What's the weather like?
B. It's _____.

[14–18]

A. What's the weather forecast?
B. There's going to be { ___[14]___ .
{ a ___[15–18]___ .

[20–26]

A. How's the weather?
B. It's ___[22–26]___ .
A. What's the temperature?
B. It's . . . degrees ___[20–21]___ .

What's the weather like today? What's the temperature?   What's the weather forecast for tomorrow?

CARDINAL NUMBERS

NIMEWO KI ENDIKE KANTITE

0 zero	**11** eleven	**21** twenty-one	**101**	one hundred (and) one
1 one	**12** twelve	**22** twenty-two	**102**	one hundred (and) two
2 two	**13** thirteen	**30** thirty	**1,000**	one thousand
3 three	**14** fourteen	**40** forty	**10,000**	ten thousand
4 four	**15** fifteen	**50** fifty	**100,000**	one hundred thousand
5 five	**16** sixteen	**60** sixty	**1,000,000**	one million
6 six	**17** seventeen	**70** seventy	**1,000,000,000**	one billion
7 seven	**18** eighteen	**80** eighty		
8 eight	**19** nineteen	**90** ninety		
9 nine	**20** twenty	**100** one hundred		
10 ten				

A. How old are you?
B. I'm _____ years old.

A. How many people are there in your family?
B. _____.

How many students are there in your class?

How many people are there in your country?

NIMEWO KI ENDIKE LÒD RANJMAN

1st	first	**11th**	eleventh	**21st**	twenty-first	**101st**	one hundred (and) first
2nd	second	**12th**	twelfth	**22nd**	twenty-second	**102nd**	one hundred (and) second
3rd	third	**13th**	thirteenth	**30th**	thirtieth	**1,000th**	one thousandth
4th	fourth	**14th**	fourteenth	**40th**	fortieth	**10,000th**	ten thousandth
5th	fifth	**15th**	fifteenth	**50th**	fiftieth	**100,000th**	one hundred thousandth
6th	sixth	**16th**	sixteenth	**60th**	sixtieth	**1,000,000th**	one millionth
7th	seventh	**17th**	seventeenth	**70th**	seventieth	**1,000,000,000th**	one billionth
8th	eighth	**18th**	eighteenth	**80th**	eightieth		
9th	ninth	**19th**	nineteenth	**90th**	ninetieth		
10th	tenth	**20th**	twentieth	**100th**	one hundredth		

A. What floor do you live on?
B. I live on the _____ floor.

A. Is this your first trip to our country?
B. No. It's my _____ trip.

What were the names of your teachers in elementary school?
(My *first*-grade teacher was Ms./Mrs./Mr. . . .)

TIME

LÈ

two o'clock

two fifteen/
a quarter after *two*

two thirty/
half past *two*

two forty-five/
a quarter to *three*

two oh five

two twenty/
twenty after *two*

two forty/
twenty to *three*

two fifty-five/
five to *three*

A. What time is it?
B. It's _____.

A. What time does the movie begin?
B. At _____.

two A.M.

two P.M.

noon /
twelve noon

midnight /
twelve midnight

A. When does the train leave?
B. At _____.

A. What time will we arrive?
B. At _____.

Tell about your daily schedule:
  What do you do? When?
  (I get up at _____. I ....)

Tell about the use of time in different cultures or countries you know:
  Do people arrive on time for work? appointments? parties?
  Do trains and buses operate exactly on schedule?
  Do movies and sports events begin on time?
  Do workplaces use time clocks or timesheets to record employees' work hours?

PYÈS LAJAN

Name	Value	Written as:	
1 penny	one cent	1¢	$ .01
2 nickel	five cents	5¢	$ .05
3 dime	ten cents	10¢	$ .10
4 quarter	twenty-five cents	25¢	$ .25
5 half dollar	fifty cents	50¢	$ .50
6 silver dollar	one dollar		$1.00

A. How much is a **penny** worth?
B. A **penny** is worth **one cent**.

A. *Soda* costs *ninety-five cents*.
Do you have enough change?
B. Yes. I have a/two/three ____(s) and . . . .

PAPYE LAJAN

Name	We sometimes say:	Value	Written as:
1 (one-) dollar bill	a one	one dollar	$ 1.00
2 five-dollar bill	a five	five dollars	$ 5.00
3 ten-dollar bill	a ten	ten dollars	$ 10.00
4 twenty-dollar bill	a twenty	twenty dollars	$ 20.00
5 fifty-dollar bill	a fifty	fifty dollars	$ 50.00
6 (one-) hundred dollar bill	a hundred	one hundred dollars	$ 100.00

A. Do you have any cash?
B. Yes. I have a **twenty-dollar bill**.

A. Can you change a **five-dollar bill**?
B. Yes. I have *five one-dollar bills*.

Written as:	We say:
$1.30	a dollar and thirty cents
	a dollar thirty
$2.50	two dollars and fifty cents
	two fifty
$56.49	fifty-six dollars and forty-nine cents
	fifty-six forty-nine

Tell about some things you usually buy.
What do they cost?

Name and describe the coins and currency in your country.
What are they worth in U.S. dollars?

ALMANNAK LA

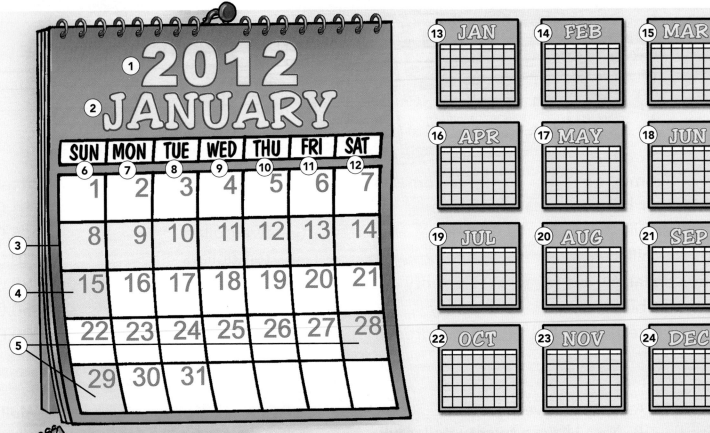

- 1. 2012
- 2. JANUARY
- 6. SUN
- 7. MON
- 8. TUE
- 9. WED
- 10. THU
- 11. FRI
- 12. SAT

JAN	FEB	MAR
13	14	15

APR	MAY	JUN
16	17	18

JUL	AUG	SEP
19	20	21

OCT	NOV	DEC
22	23	24

25. 1/3/12 — JAN 3 2012

26. HAPPY 25th

27.

28. APPOINTMENT

Charles Wong, M.D.

Date: February 21

Time: 3:00 PM

ane	1	year
mwa	2	month
semèn/semenn	3	week
jou	4	day
wikenn	5	weekend

Jou Semèn yo — **Days of the Week**

dimanch	6	Sunday
lendi	7	Monday
madi	8	Tuesday
mèkredi	9	Wednesday
jedi	10	Thursday
vandredi	11	Friday
samdi	12	Saturday

Mwa nan Anne yo — **Months of the Year**

janvye	13	January
fevriye	14	February
mas	15	March
avril	16	April
me	17	May
jen	18	June
jiyè	19	July
out	20	August
septanm	21	September
oktòb	22	October
novanm	23	November
desanm	24	December

3 janvye 2012	25	January 3, 2012
twa janvye de mil douz		January third, two thousand twelve
fèt	26	birthday
anivèsè	27	anniversary
randevou	28	appointment

A. What year is it?
B. It's _____.

[13–24]
A. What month is it?
B. It's _____.

[6–12]
A. What day is it?
B. It's _____.

A. What's today's date?
B. It's _____.

[26–28]
A. When is your _____?
B. It's on _____.

Which days of the week do you go to work / school?
(I go to work / school on _____.)

What is your date of birth?
(I was born on ...*month day, year*....)

What's your favorite day of the week? Why?

What's your favorite month of the year? Why?

EKSPRESYON LÈ AK SEZON

yè	**1**	yesterday
jodiya	**2**	today
demen	**3**	tomorrow
maten	**4**	morning
apremidi	**5**	afternoon
aswè	**6**	evening
lannwit	**7**	night
yè maten	**8**	yesterday morning
yè apremidi	**9**	yesterday afternoon
yè swa	**10**	yesterday evening
yè swa	**11**	last night
maten an	**12**	this morning
apremidi a	**13**	this afternoon
aswè a	**14**	this evening
aswè a	**15**	tonight
demen maten	**16**	tomorrow morning
demen apremidi	**17**	tomorrow afternoon
demen swa	**18**	tomorrow evening
demen swa	**19**	tomorrow night

semenn pase	**20**	last week
semenn sa a	**21**	this week
semenn pwochèn	**22**	next week
yon fwa pa semenn	**23**	once a week
de fwa pa semenn	**24**	twice a week
twa fwa pa semenn	**25**	three times a week
chak jou	**26**	every day

Sezon Yo **Seasons**

prentan	**27**	spring
lete	**28**	summer
lotòn	**29**	fall / autumn
livè	**30**	winter

What did you do yesterday morning/afternoon/evening?

What did you do last night?

What are you going to do tomorrow morning/afternoon/evening/night?

What did you do last week?

What are your plans for next week?

How many times a week do you have English class?/go to the supermarket?/exercise?

What's your favorite season? Why?

TYPES OF HOUSING AND COMMUNITIES

KALITE LOJMAN AK KOMINOTE YO

bilding ak apatman	**1**	apartment building	pansyon pou granmoun	**8** nursing home
kay	**2**	house	abri/kay pwovizwa	**9** shelter
kay an 2 apatman	**3**	duplex/two-family house	fèm	**10** farm
			ranch	**11** ranch
kay kole	**4**	townhouse/ townhome	kaybato	**12** houseboat
kondo	**5**	condominium/condo	vil la	**13** the city
dòtwa	**6**	dormitory/dorm	zòn andeyò lavil	**14** the suburbs
trelè	**7**	mobile home	peyi a	**15** the country
			ti vil/vilaj	**16** a town/village

A. Where do you live?

B. I live
{ in a/an ___[1–9]___.
  on a ___[10–12]___.
  in ___[13–16]___. }

[1–12]

A. Town Taxi Company.
B. Hello. Please send a taxi to ......(address)......
A. Is that a house or an apartment building?
B. It's a/an _____.
A. All right. We'll be there right away.

[1–12]

A. This is the Emergency Operator.
B. Please send an ambulance to ......(address)......
A. Is that a private home?
B. It's a/an _____.
A. What's your name and telephone number?
B. ....

Tell about people you know and where they live.

Discuss:
Who lives in dormitories?
Who lives in nursing homes?
Who lives in shelters?
Why?

etajè liv	**1**	bookcase	wopalè	**16**	speaker
pòtre/foto	**2**	picture/ photograph	aparèy estereyo	**17**	stereo system
tablo	**3**	painting	mèb pou kenbe magazin	**18**	magazine holder
tab chemine	**4**	mantel			
chemine	**5**	fireplace	zòrye/kousen	**19**	pillow
ekran chemine	**6**	fireplace screen	sofa/kannape	**20**	sofa/couch
aparèy DVD	**7**	DVD player	plant	**21**	plant
televizyon	**8**	television/TV	tab salon	**22**	coffee table
VCR/anrejistrè kasèt-videyo	**9**	VCR/video cassette recorder	tapi	**23**	rug
			lanp	**24**	lamp
mi	**10**	wall	abajou	**25**	lampshade
plafon	**11**	ceiling	tab lanp	**26**	end table
rido	**12**	drapes	planche	**27**	floor
fenèt	**13**	window	lanp kanpe atè	**28**	floor lamp
sofa 2 plas	**14**	loveseat	fotèy	**29**	armchair
zòn anmizman	**15**	wall unit			

A. Where are you?
B. I'm in the living room.
A. What are you doing?
B. I'm dusting* the **bookcase**.

*dusting/cleaning

A. You have a very nice living room!
B. Thank you.
A. Your _____ is/are beautiful!
B. Thank you for saying so.

A. Uh-oh! I just spilled coffee on your _____!
B. That's okay. Don't worry about it.

Tell about your living room.
(In my living room there's ....)

THE DINING ROOM

SALAMANJE A

tab salamanje	**1**	(dining room) table	pòtbouji	**18**	candlestick
chèz salamanje	**2**	(dining room) chair	plat	**19**	platter
pàntyè/gadmanje	**3**	buffet	berye	**20**	butter dish
kabare	**4**	tray	salyè	**21**	salt shaker
teyè	**5**	teapot	pwavrye	**22**	pepper shaker
kafetyè	**6**	coffee pot	nap	**23**	tablecloth
sikriye	**7**	sugar bowl	sèvyèt tab	**24**	napkin
pòtkrèm	**8**	creamer	fouchèt	**25**	fork
po/podlo/pòtao	**9**	pitcher	asyèt	**26**	plate
chandelye	**10**	chandelier	kouto	**27**	knife
veselye	**11**	china cabinet	kiyè	**28**	spoon
vesèl pòslèn	**12**	china	bòl	**29**	bowl
bòl salad	**13**	salad bowl	gode	**30**	mug
bòl sèvis	**14**	serving bowl	vè	**31**	glass
asyèt pou sèvi	**15**	serving dish	tas	**32**	cup
po flè	**16**	vase	soukoup	**33**	saucer
bouji	**17**	candle			

A. This **dining room table** is very nice.
B. Thank you. It was a gift from my *grandmother.**

*grandmother/grandfather/aunt/uncle/. . .

[In a store]

A. May I help you?
B. Yes, please. Do you have _____s?*
A. Yes. _____s* are right over there.
B. Thank you.

*With 12, use the singular.

[At home]

A. Where did you get this old _____?
B. At a yard sale. How do you like it?
A. It's VERY unusual!

Tell about your dining room.
(In my dining room there's
.............)

THE BEDROOM

CHANMAKOUCHE A

kabann	**1**	bed	rido	**13**	curtains
tèt kabann	**2**	headboard	lanp	**14**	lamp
zòrye	**3**	pillow	revèy	**15**	alarm clock
tèdoreye	**4**	pillowcase	radyo revèy	**16**	clock radio
dra	**5**	sheet	tab dennwit	**17**	night table/ nightstand
lenn	**6**	blanket			
lenn elektrik	**7**	electric blanket	glas/miwa	**18**	mirror
kouvreli	**8**	bedspread	bwat bijou	**19**	jewelry box
kouvreli matlase	**9**	comforter/quilt	kwafèz	**20**	dresser/bureau
tapi	**10**	carpet	matla	**21**	mattress
komòd	**11**	chest (of drawers)	matla ak resò	**22**	box spring
pèsyèn	**12**	blinds	kare kabann	**23**	bed frame

A. Ooh! Look at that big bug!
B. Where?
A. It's on the **bed**!
B. I'll get it.

[In a store]
A. Excuse me. I'm looking for a/an _____.*
B. We have some very nice _____s, and they're all on sale this week!
A. Oh, good!

* With 12 & 13, use: Excuse me. I'm looking for ____.

[In a bedroom]
A. Oh, no! I just lost my contact lens!
B. Where?
A. I think it's on the _____.
B. I'll help you look.

Tell about your bedroom.
(In my bedroom there's ....)

THE KITCHEN

KWIZIN NAN

frijidè	**1** refrigerator	wobinè/tiyo	**11** faucet	kafetyè pou te	**23** tea kettle
frizè	**2** freezer	evye	**12** sink	founo	**24** stove/range
poubèl/	**3** garbage	machin vesèl	**13** dishwasher	fou	**25** oven
bwat fatra	pail	moulen	**14** (garbage)	tostè	**26** toaster
batèz	**4** (electric)	dechè	disposal	kafetyè	**27** coffeemaker
elektrik	mixer	tòchon vesèl	**15** dish towel	konpresè	**28** trash
plaka	**5** cabinet	panyen asyèt	**16** dish rack	fatra	compactor
sipò tòchon	**6** paper towel	etajè epis	**17** spice rack	planchèt pou	**29** cutting
papye	holder	ouvbwat	**18** (electric)	dekoupe	board
kanistè	**7** canister	eletrik	can opener	liv kwizin	**30** cookbook
kontwa kuizin	**8** counter	blenndè	**19** blender	aparèy moulen	**31** food
savon vesèl	**9** dishwasher	fou pou griye/	**20** toaster	manje	processor
an poud	detergent	fou tostè	oven	chèz kwizin	**32** kitchen chair
savon vesèl	**10** dishwashing	maykowev	**21** microwave	tab kwizin	**33** kitchen table
likid	liquid	tòchon chodyè	**22** potholder	napwon	**34** placemat

A. I think we need a new **refrigerator**.
B. I think you're right.

[In a store]
A. Excuse me. Are your _____s still on sale?
B. Yes, they are. They're twenty percent off.

[In a kitchen]
A. When did you get this/these new _____(s)?
B. I got it/them last week.

Tell about your kitchen.
(In my kitchen there's ....)

THE BABY'S ROOM

CHANM BEBE A

nounous	**1**	teddy bear	tchatcha	**15** rattle
monitè pou bebe/ entèkòm	**2**	baby monitor/ intercom	twotinèt	**16** walker
komòd	**3**	chest (of drawers)	bèso	**17** cradle
bèso/kabann bebe	**4**	crib	pousèt bebe	**18** stroller
jwèt mobil	**5**	mobile	vwati bebe	**19** baby carriage
tab pou chanje kouchèt	**6**	changing table	chèz bebe pou machin	**20** car seat/ safety seat
salopèt bebe	**7**	stretch suit	vwati bebe	**21** baby carrier
poubèl pou kouchèt	**8**	diaper pail	asyèt bebe	**22** food warmer
			chèz pou wose bebe	**23** booster seat
neyèz	**9**	night light	chèz bebe	**24** baby seat
bwat jwèt	**10**	toy chest	chèz wo pou bebe	**25** high chair
jwèt boure	**11**	stuffed animal	bèso pliyan	**26** portable crib
pope	**12**	doll	vaz bebe	**27** potty
balanswa	**13**	swing	sakavant pou bebe	**28** baby frontpack
pak bebe	**14**	playpen	sakado pou bebe	**29** baby backpack

A. Thank you for the **teddy bear**. It's a very nice gift.
B. You're welcome.

A. That's a very nice _____.
   Where did you get it?
B. It was a gift from ....

A. Do you have everything you need
   before the baby comes?
B. Almost everything. We're still looking
   for a/an _____ and a/an _____.

Tell about your country:
   What things do people buy for a new baby?
   Does a new baby sleep in a separate room,
   as in the United States?

THE BATHROOM

SALDEBEN AN

poubèl	**1**	wastebasket	sèvyèt	**17**	towel
bifèt twalèt	**2**	vanity	pòtsèvyèt	**18**	towel rack
savon	**3**	soap	ponp watè	**19**	plunger
savonye	**4**	soap dish	bwòs twalèt	**20**	toilet brush
ponp savon likid	**5**	soap dispenser	papye ijyenik	**21**	toilet paper
lavabo	**6**	sink	santibon pou twalèt	**22**	air freshener
wobinèt/tiyo	**7**	faucet	watè	**23**	toilet
bifèt medikaman	**8**	medicine cabinet	rebò watè	**24**	toilet seat
glas/miwa	**9**	mirror	douch	**25**	shower
tas	**10**	cup	rido douch	**26**	shower curtain
bwòsdan	**11**	toothbrush	benywa/basen	**27**	bathtub/tub
bwòsdan elektrik	**12**	electric toothbrush	tapi kawotchou	**28**	rubber mat
sechwa cheve	**13**	hair dryer	tiyo drenaj	**29**	drain
etajè	**14**	shelf	eponj	**30**	sponge
panyen rad sal	**15**	hamper	tapi saldeben	**31**	bath mat
vantilatè	**16**	fan	balans	**32**	scale

A. Where's the **hair dryer**?
B. It's *on* the **vanity**.

A. Where's the **soap**?
B. It's *in* the **soap dish**.

A. Where's the **plunger**?
B. It's *next to* the **toilet brush**.

A. [Knock. Knock.] Did I leave my glasses in there?
B. Yes. They're on/in/next to the _____.

A. *Bobby*? You didn't clean up the bathroom! There's toothpaste on the _____, and there's powder all over the _____!
B. Sorry. I'll clean it up right away.

Tell about your bathroom.
(In my bathroom there's ....)

OUTSIDE THE HOME

DEYÒ KAY LA

Lakou Devan		Front Yard	Lakou Dèyè		Backyard
poto limyè	**1**	lamppost	chèz long/gazon	**15**	lawn chair
bwat lapòs	**2**	mailbox	tondèz gazon	**16**	lawnmower
eskalye devan	**3**	front steps	depo zouti	**17**	tool shed
galri devan kay	**4**	front porch	pòt til	**18**	screen door
pòt siklòn	**5**	storm door	pòt dèyè	**19**	back door
pòt devan	**6**	front door	manch pòt	**20**	door knob
sonnèt	**7**	doorbell	teras an bwa	**21**	deck
fennèt	**8**	window	recho griyad	**22**	barbecue/grill
til nan fenèt	**9**	window screen	pasyo	**23**	patio
pèsyèn	**10**	shutter	antèn parabolik	**24**	satellite dish
twati/dokay	**11**	roof	antèn	**25**	TV antenna
garaj	**12**	garage	chemine	**26**	chimney
pòt garaj	**13**	garage door	pòt sou kote	**27**	side door
ale garaj	**14**	driveway	kloti	**28**	fence

A. When are you going to repair the **lamppost**?
B. I'm going to repair it next Saturday.

[On the telephone]
A. Harry's Home Repairs.
B. Hello. Do you fix _____s?
A. No, we don't.
B. Oh, okay. Thank you.

[At work on Monday morning]
A. What did you do this weekend?
B. Nothing much. I repaired my _____ and my _____.

Do you like to repair things?
What things can you repair yourself?
What things can't you repair? Who repairs them?

BILDING AK APATMAN I

Sèche apatman	**Looking for an Apartment**	**Pran lojman**	**Moving In**	eskalye ijans	**19**	fire escape
seksyon reklam apatman/ nan jounal	**1** apartment ads/ classified ads	kamyon k ap bwote	**8** moving truck/ moving van	garaj	**20**	parking garage
				balkon	**21**	balcony
lis apatman ki nan piblisite	**2** apartment listings	vwazen	**9** neighbor	lakou	**22**	courtyard
		jeran	**10** building manager	pakin	**23**	parking lot
siy kay ki vid	**3** vacancy sign			plas pakin	**24**	parking space
		jeran baryè	**11** doorman			
Siyen yon kontra	**Signing a Lease**	kle	**12** key	pisin	**25**	swimming pool
lokatè	**4** tenant	seri	**13** lock			
mèt kay la	**5** landlord	premye etaj	**14** first floor	basen dlo souke	**26**	whirlpool
kontra	**6** lease	dezyèm etaj	**15** second floor			
depo	**7** security deposit	twazyèm etaj	**16** third floor	panye fatra	**27**	trash bin
		katriyèm etaj	**17** fourth floor	klimatizè	**28**	air conditioner
		twati/dokay	**18** roof			

[19–28]
A. Is there a **fire escape**?
B. Yes, there is.

[14–17]
A. What floor is the apartment on?
B. It's on the _____.

[20, 22–27]
A. Where's the _____?
B. It's in back of the building.

How do people look for apartments in your city or town?

Tell about an apartment building you know:
How many floors are there?
Is there an elevator?
Is there a parking lot or parking garage?
How many apartments are there in the building?

BILDING AK APATMAN II

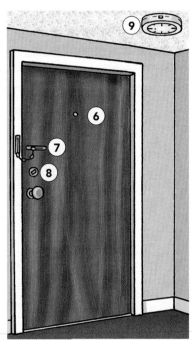

Antre	**Lobby**
entèkòm	**1** intercom
sonnèt	**2** buzzer
bwat lapòs	**3** mailbox
elevatè	**4** elevator
eskalye	**5** stairway

Pòt Antre	**Doorway**
pòt ak twou jouda	**6** peephole
chenn pòt	**7** door chain
seri	**8** lock
alam pou lafimen	**9** smoke detector

Koulwa	**Hallway**
ekzit pou epanye dife/ eskalye ijan	**10** fire exit/emergency stairway
alam dife	**11** fire alarm
jeran	**12** superintendent
sistèm awozaj	**13** sprinkler system
twou fatra	**14** garbage chute/ trash chute

Besment	**Basement**
depo	**15** storage room
kazye	**16** storage locker
sal lesiv	**17** laundry room
baryè sekirite	**18** security gate

[1, 4]
A. Is there an **intercom**?
B. Yes, there is.

[2, 3, 5–18]
A. Is there a **mailbox**?
B. Yes, there is.

[Renting an apartment]
A. Let me show you around.
B. Okay.
A. This is the _____, and here's the _____.
B. I see.

[On the telephone]
A. Mom and Dad? I found an apartment.
B. Good. Tell us about it.
A. It has a/an _____ and a/an _____.
B. That's nice. Does it have a/an _____?
A. Yes, it does.

Do you or someone you know live in an apartment building? Tell about it.

PWOBLÈM KAY AK REPARASYON I

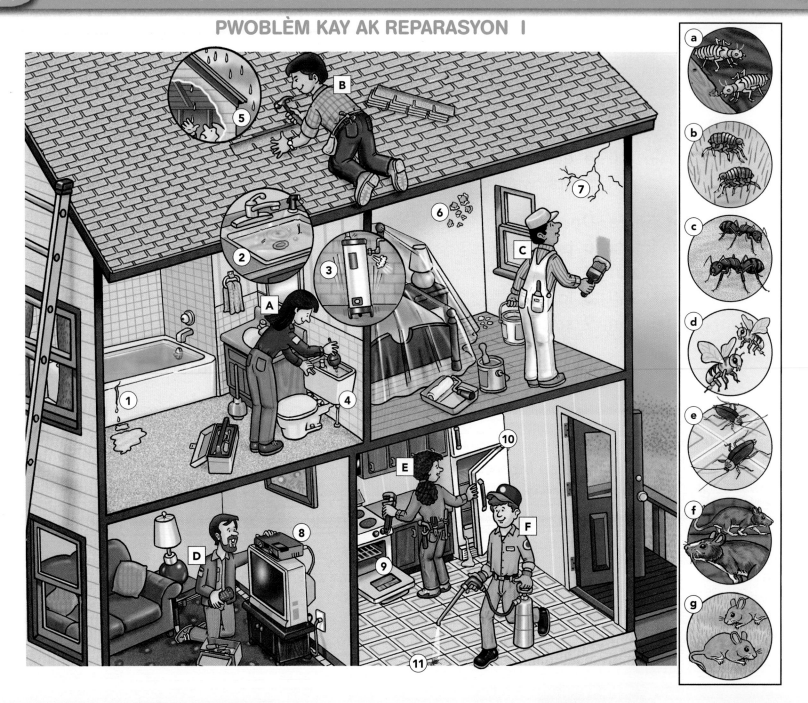

plonbye A plumber
Benywa ap koule. **1** The bathtub is leaking.

Lavabo a bouche. **2** The sink is clogged.
Dlo cho a pap travay. **3** The hot water heater isn't working.

Twalèt la kraze. **4** The toilet is broken.

bòs twati B roofer
Do kay la koule. **5** The roof is leaking.

(kay) pent C (house) painter
Penti a ap dekale. **6** The paint is peeling.
Mi an fann/pete. **7** The wall is cracked.

konpanyi pou D cable TV company
televizyon
Kab televizyon an **8** The cable TV isn't pap travay. working.

bòs tout metye E appliance repairperson
Fou a pap travay. **9** The stove isn't working.
Frijidè a kraze. **10** The refrigerator is broken.

ekstèminatè F exterminator/ pest control specialist
Geneyn ___ nan kizin/ **11** There are ___ in the kitchen.
kuizin nan.
foumi bwa **a** termites
pis **b** fleas
foumi **c** ants
myèl **d** bees
ravèt **e** cockroaches
rat **f** rats
sourit **g** mice

A. What's the matter?
B. ___[1–11]___ .
A. I think we should call a/an ___[A–F]___ .

[1–11]
A. I'm having a problem in my apartment/house.
B. What's the problem?
A. _____ .

[A–F]
A. Can you recommend a good _____?
B. Yes. You should call ....

What do you do when you have these problems in your home? Do you fix things yourself, or do you call someone?

serirye	**A**	**locksmith**
Seri a kraze.	**1**	The lock is broken.

elektrisyen	**B**	**electrician**
Limyè devan an pa limen.	**2**	The front light doesn't go on.
Sonèt la pa travay.	**3**	The doorbell doesn't ring.
Pa gen kouran nan salon an.	**4**	The power is out in the living room.

netwayè chemine	**C**	**chimneysweep**
Chemine a sal.	**5**	The chimney is dirty.

bòs tout metye	**D**	**home repairperson/ "handyman"**
Mozayik nan twalèt la sekwe.	**6**	The tiles in the bathroom are loose.

chapantye	**E**	**carpenter**
Eskalye yo kraze.	**7**	The steps are broken.
Pòt la pa louvri.	**8**	The door doesn't open.

sèvis chofaj ak è kondisyone	**F**	**heating and air conditioning service**
Chalè nan sistèm nan p ap mache.	**9**	The heating system is broken.
Èkondisyone a p ap travay.	**10**	The air conditioning isn't working.

A. What's the matter?
B. __[1–10]__ .
A. I think we should call a/an __[A–F]__ .

[1–10]
A. I'm having a problem in my apartment/house.
B. What's the problem?
A. _____ .

[A–F]
A. Can you recommend a good _____?
B. Yes. You should call ....

What do you do when you have these problems in your home? Do you fix things yourself, or do you call someone?

CLEANING YOUR HOME

NETWAYE KAY OU

bale atè a	**A**	sweep the floor
pase vakyòm	**B**	vacuum
mòp atè a	**C**	mop the floor
lave fennèt yo	**D**	wash the windows
siye	**E**	dust
sire atè a	**F**	wax the floor
poli mèb yo	**G**	polish the furniture
netwaye saldeben an	**H**	clean the bathroom
mete fatra a deyò	**I**	take out the garbage

bale	**1**	broom
ranmaswa	**2**	dustpan
epousèt	**3**	whisk broom
bale pou tapi	**4**	carpet sweeper
vakyòm/aspirate	**5**	vacuum (cleaner)
pyès pou aspiratè	**6**	vacuum cleaner attachments
sak vakyòm	**7**	vacuum cleaner bag
vakyòm ak men	**8**	hand vacuum

mòp pou netwaye pousyè/ mòp seche	**9**	(dust) mop/ (dry) mop
mòp eponj	**10**	(sponge) mop
mòp mouye	**11**	(wet) mop
tòchon papye	**12**	paper towels
likid pou netwaye fennèt	**13**	window cleaner
amonyak	**14**	ammonia
twal epouste/chifon	**15**	dust cloth
bale an plim	**16**	feather duster
likid pou sire planch	**17**	floor wax
poli pou mèb	**18**	furniture polish
bagay pou netwaye	**19**	cleanser
bwòs netwayaj	**20**	scrub brush
eponj	**21**	sponge
bokit	**22**	bucket/pail
bwat fatra	**23**	trash can/ garbage can
kès pou bwat fèblan	**24**	recycling bin

[A–I]
A. What are you doing?
B. I'm **sweep**ing **the floor**.

[1–24]
A. I can't find the **broom**.
B. Look over there!

[1–12, 15, 16, 20–24]
A. Excuse me. Do you sell _____(s)?
B. Yes. They're at the back of the store.
A. Thanks.

[13, 14, 17–19]
A. Excuse me. Do you sell _____?
B. Yes. It's at the back of the store.
A. Thanks.

What household cleaning chores do people do in your home? What things do they use?

ZOUTI AK FOUNITI NAN KAY

mato	**1** hammer		bourèt	**16** wheelbarrow
si	**2** saw		tiyo awozaj	**17** hose
tounvis	**3** screwdriver		bale fè	**18** rake
kle plat	**4** wrench		yad an bwa	**19** yardstick
kle tiyo	**5** monkey wrench		flach	**20** flashlight
eto	**6** vise		nechèl	**21** ladder
pens/tennay	**7** pliers		chasmouch	**22** fly swatter
bwat zouti	**8** toolbox		ponp	**23** plunger
dril elektrik	**9** electric drill		sourisye	**24** mousetrap
klou	**10** nail		ensèktisid	**25** bug spray/ insect spray
wondèl	**11** washer		pil	**26** batteries
ekwou	**12** nut		anpoul elektrik	**27** lightbulbs/bulbs
ekwou	**13** screw		penti	**28** paint
boulon	**14** bolt		penso	**29** paintbrush/brush
pèl	**15** shovel		woulo pou penti	**30** paint roller

A. I can't find the **hammer**!
B. Look in the utility cabinet.
A. Okay. Thanks.

* With 10–14, use: I can't find any _____s.

[1–9, 15–25, 29, 30]
A. Can I borrow your _____?
B. Sure.
A. Thanks.

[10–14, 26, 27]
A. Can I borrow some _____(s)?
B. Sure.
A. Thanks.

What tools and home supplies do you have? How and when do you use them?

DIVÈS KOTE NAN LAVIL LA I

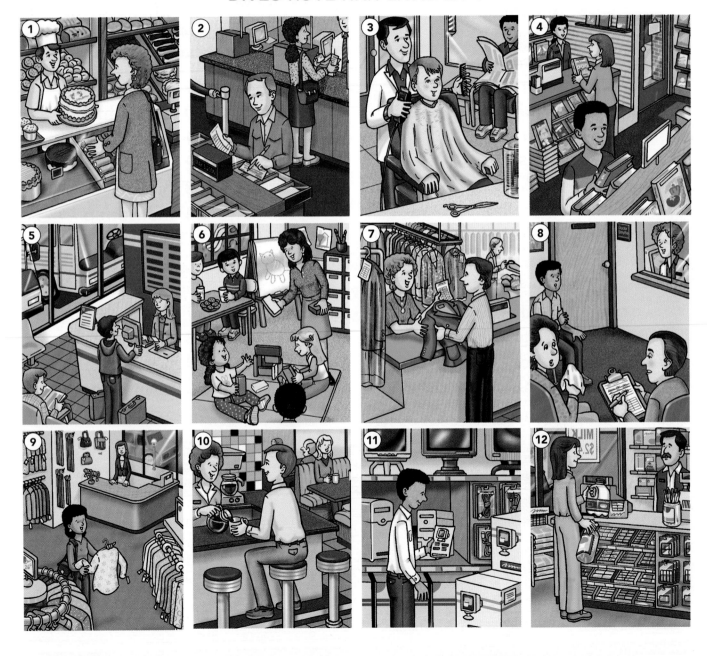

boulanjri	**1**	bakery
bank	**2**	bank
kwafè	**3**	barber shop
magazen liv	**4**	book store
estasyon bis	**5**	bus station
gadri	**6**	child-care center/ day-care center
drayklining	**7**	cleaners
klinik	**8**	clinic
magazen rad	**9**	clothing store
magazen pou manje leje	**10**	coffee shop
magazen konpitè	**11**	computer store
boutik asòti	**12**	convenience store

A. Where are you going?
B. I'm going to the **bakery**.

A. Are you going to the _____?
B. No. I'm going to the _____.

A. Where did you go?
B. I went to the _____.

Which of these places are in your neighborhood?
(In my neighborhood there's a/an ....)

DIVÈS KOTE NAN LAVIL LA II

magazen varyete	**1**	department store
magazen bon mache	**2**	discount store
ba dounòt	**3**	donut shop
famasi	**4**	drug store/pharmacy
magazen elektwonik	**5**	electronics store
sant pou swen zye	**6**	eye-care center/optician
restoran manje prese	**7**	fast-food restaurant
magazen flè	**8**	flower shop/florist
magazen mèb	**9**	furniture store
estasyon gazolin	**10**	gas station/service station
episri	**11**	grocery store
salondbote	**12**	hair salon

A. Hi! How are you today?
B. Fine. Where are you going?
A. To the **department store**. How about you?
B. I'm going to the **discount store**.

A. I'm going to the _____.
B. See you later.
A. Bye.

A. Did you go to the _____ today?
B. No. I went to the _____.

Which of these places are in your neighborhood?
(In my neighborhood there's a/an …………)

PLACES AROUND TOWN III

DIVÈS KOTE NAN LAVIL LA III

magazen kenkay	**1**	hardware store
klib egzèsis	**2**	health club
lopital	**3**	hospital
otèl	**4**	hotel
boutik krèmalaglas	**5**	ice cream shop
blanchisri otomatik	**6**	laundromat
bibliyotèk	**7**	library
magazen fanm ansent	**8**	maternity shop
motèl	**9**	motel
sinema	**10**	movie theater
magazen mizik	**11**	music store
estidyo maniki ak pediki	**12**	nail salon

A. Where's the **hardware store**?
B. It's right over there.

A. Excuse me. Where's the _____?
B. It's around the corner.
A. Thank you.

A. Excuse me. Is this the way to the _____?
B. Yes, it is.
A. Thanks.

Which of these places are in your neighborhood? (In my neighborhood there's a/an ....)

DIVÈS KOTE NAN LAVIL LA IV

pak	**1**	park	magazen soulye	**7**	shoe store
magazen atik	**2**	pet shop	sant komès	**8**	(shopping) mall
bèt kay			sipèmakèt	**9**	supermarket
boutik pitza	**3**	pizza shop	magazen jwèt	**10**	toy store
lapòs	**4**	post office	estasyon tren	**11**	train station
restoran	**5**	restaurant	magazen videyo	**12**	video store
lekòl	**6**	school			

A. Is there a **park** nearby?
B. Yes. There's a **park** around the corner.

A. Excuse me. Is there a _____ near here?
B. Yes, there is. There's a _____ right over there.
A. Thank you.

A. Oh, no! I can't find my wallet/purse!
B. Did you leave it at the _____?
A. Maybe I did.

Which of these places are in your neighborhood?
(In my neighborhood there's a/an ....)

THE CITY I

LAVIL LA I

tribinal	**1** courthouse	prizon	**12** jail
taksi/laliy	**2** taxi/cab	twotwa	**13** sidewalk
estasyon taksi	**3** taxi stand	lari	**14** street
chofè taksi/	**4** taxi driver/	limyè lari	**15** street light
chofè laliy	cab driver	plas pakin	**16** parking lot
tiyo ponpye	**5** fire hydrant	kontwolè kontè pakin	**17** meter maid
panyen fatra	**6** trash container	kontè pakin	**18** parking meter
meri/lakomin	**7** city hall	kamyon fatra	**19** garbage truck
bwat sonnètpou dife	**8** fire alarm box	sòbwe	**20** subway
bwat postal/bwat lèt	**9** mailbox	estasyon sòbwe	**21** subway station
devèswa egou	**10** sewer		
estasyon polis	**11** police station		

A. Where's the _____?
B. On/In/Next to/Between/Across from/
In front of/Behind/Under/Over the _____.

[1, 11, 12]
A. Excuse me. Where's the _____?
B. It's around the corner.

[3, 6, 8, 9, 16, 21]
A. Excuse me. Is there a _____ nearby?
B. Yes. There's a _____ down the street.

Which of these people, places, and things are in your neighborhood?

THE CITY II

LAVIL LA II

boutik jounal	**1** newsstand		estasyon ponpye	**10** fire station
limyè trafik	**2** traffic light		estasyon bis	**11** bus stop
kalfou	**3** intersection		bis	**12** bus
ajan lapolis/ jandam	**4** police officer		chofè bis	**13** bus driver
pasaj pyeton	**5** crosswalk		bilding pou biwo	**14** office building
pyeton	**6** pedestrian		telefòn piblik	**15** public telephone
kamyon krèm	**7** ice cream truck		ansèy lari	**16** street sign
rebò twotwa	**8** curb		twou egou	**17** manhole
pakin ann etaj	**9** parking garage		motosiklèt	**18** motorcycle
			machann sou twotwa	**19** street vendor
			gichè pou machin	**20** drive-through window

A. Where's the _____?
B. On/In/Next to/Between/Across from/ In front of/Behind/Under/Over the _____.

[4, 13, 19]
A. What do you do?
B. I'm a _____.

[1, 5, 7, 9–11, 14, 15]
A. Excuse me. Is there a/an _____ near here?
B. Yes. There's a/an _____ up the street.

Go to an intersection in your city or town. What do you see? Make a list. Then tell about it. (Use the words on pages 80–83.)

MOUN AK DESKRIPSYON FIZIK I

timoun-timoun yo	**1**	**child–children**	wotè	**height**
bebe	**2**	baby/infant	wo	**14** tall
ti moun k ap aprann mache	**3**	toddler	wotè mwayenn	**15** average height
			kout	**16** short
gason	**4**	boy		
fi	**5**	girl	**pwa**	**weight**
jèn	**6**	teenager	lou	**17** heavy
			pwa mwayenn	**18** average weight
granmoun	**7**	**adult**	mèg	**19** thin/slim
gason-gason yo	**8**	man–men		
fanm-fanm yo	**9**	woman–women	ansent	**20** pregnant
retrete	**10**	senior citizen		
			enfim/kokobe	**21** physically challenged
laj		**age**		
jenn	**11**	young	wè twoub	**22** vision impaired
mwayen daj	**12**	middle-aged	moun ki tande di	**23** hearing impaired
vye	**13**	old		

A. Tell me about *your brother.*
B. He's *a tall heavy boy.*

A. Tell me about *your sister.*
B. She's *a short thin girl.*

A. Can you describe the person?
B. I think so.
A. What's *his* age?
B. *He's* ___[11–13]___ .
A. What's *his* height?
B. *He's* ___[14–16]___ .
A. What's *his* weight?
B. *He's* ___[17–19]___ .

Tell about yourself.

Tell about people in your family.

PEOPLE AND PHYSICAL DESCRIPTIONS II

MOUN AK DESKRIPSYON FIZIK II

Dekri cheve	**Describing Hair**		nwa	**7** black
long	**1** long		mawon	**8** brown
longè zepòl/ rive sou zepòl	**2** shoulder length		blon	**9** blond
			wouj	**10** red
kout	**3** short		gri	**11** gray
swa	**4** straight		chòv	**12** bald
boukle (cheve)	**5** wavy		bab	**13** beard
boukle	**6** curly		moustach	**14** mustache

A. What does *your new boss* look like?
B. *She* has *long straight black* hair.

A. What does *your grandfather* look like?
B. *He* has *short curly gray* hair.

A. Can you describe *his* hair?
B. *He's bald*, and *he* has a *mustache*.

Tell about yourself.   Tell about people in your family.   Tell about your favorite actor or actress or other famous person.

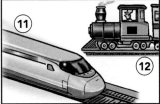

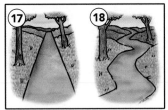

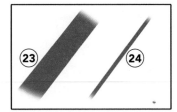

nèf/nouvo – vye	**1–2**	new – old	swa – boukle	**19–20**	straight – curly
jenn – vye	**3–4**	young – old	laj – etwat	**21–22**	wide – narrow
wo – kout	**5–6**	tall – short	pwès – mens	**23–24**	thick – thin
long – kout	**7–8**	long – short	fonse – klè	**25–26**	dark – light
gwo – ti/piti	**9–10**	large/big – small/little	wo – ba	**27–28**	high – low
rapid – dousman	**11–12**	fast – slow	lach – sere	**29–30**	loose – tight
lou/gra – mèg/chèch	**13–14**	heavy/fat – thin/skinny	bon – move	**31–32**	good – bad
lou – lejè	**15–16**	heavy – light	cho – frèt	**33–34**	hot – cold
dwa – kwochi	**17–18**	straight – crooked	annòd – andezòd	**35–36**	neat – messy

[1–2]
A. Is your car **new**?
B. No. It's **old**.

1–2	Is your car _____?	13–14	Is your friend _____?	25–26	Is the room _____?
3–4	Is he _____?	15–16	Is the box _____?	27–28	Is the bridge _____?
5–6	Is your sister _____?	17–18	Is the road _____?	29–30	Are the pants _____?
7–8	Is his hair _____?	19–20	Is her hair _____?	31–32	Are your neighbor's children _____?
9–10	Is their dog _____?	21–22	Is the tie _____?	33–34	Is the water _____?
11–12	Is the train _____?	23–24	Is the line _____?	35–36	Is your desk _____?

A. Tell me about your ....
B. He's/She's/It's/They're ____.

A. Do you have a/an ____ ....?
B. No. I have a/an ____ ....

Describe yourself.
Describe a person you know.
Describe some things in your home.
Describe some things in your community.

DESKRIPSYON MOUN AK BAGAY II

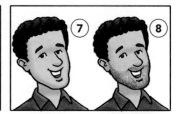

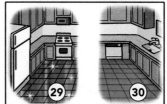

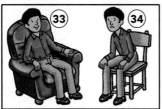

fasil – difisil/di	**1–2**	easy – difficult/hard
mou – di	**3–4**	soft – hard
pwòp – sal	**5–6**	clean – dirty
vlou – graj	**7–8**	smooth – rough
gwo bwi/eskandal – trankil/pezib	**9–10**	noisy/loud – quiet
marye – selibatè	**11–12**	married – single
rich – pòv	**13–14**	rich/wealthy – poor
bèl – lèd	**15–16**	pretty/beautiful – ugly
bèl gason – lèd	**17–18**	handsome – ugly
mouye – sèk	**19–20**	wet – dry
louvri – fèmen	**21–22**	open – closed
plen – vid	**23–24**	full – empty
chè – bon mache	**25–26**	expensive – cheap/inexpensive
bòzò – senp	**27–28**	fancy – plain
klere – mat	**29–30**	shiny – dull
file – pa file	**31–32**	sharp – dull
alèz – pa alèz	**33–34**	comfortable – uncomfortable
onèt – malonèt	**35–36**	honest – dishonest

[1–2]
A. Is the homework **easy**?
B. No. It's **difficult**.

1–2 Is the homework _____?
3–4 Is the mattress _____?
5–6 Are the windows _____?
7–8 Is your skin _____?
9–10 Is your neighbor _____?
11–12 Is your sister _____?

13–14 Is your uncle _____?
15–16 Is the witch _____?
17–18 Is the pirate _____?
19–20 Are the clothes _____?
21–22 Is the door _____?
23–24 Is the pitcher _____?

25–26 Is that restaurant _____?
27–28 Is the dress _____?
29–30 Is your kitchen floor _____?
31–32 Is the knife _____?
33–34 Is the chair _____?
35–36 Is he _____?

A. Tell me about your ....
B. He's/She's/It's/They're ____.

A. Do you have a/an ____ ....?
B. No. I have a/an ____ ....

Describe yourself.
Describe a person you know.
Describe some things in your home.
Describe some things in your community.

bouke	**1** tired	plen	**9** full	
dòmi nanje	**2** sleepy	kontan	**10** happy	
bouke anpil	**3** exhausted	tris/kè pa kontan	**11** sad/unhappy	
malad	**4** sick/ill	mizerab	**12** miserable	
cho	**5** hot	eksite	**13** excited	
frèt	**6** cold	kontraye	**14** disappointed	
grangou	**7** hungry	vèkse	**15** upset	
swaf	**8** thirsty	annwiye	**16** annoyed	

A. You look **tired**.
B. I am. I'm VERY **tired**.

What makes you happy?   What makes you sad?   When do you get annoyed?

DESKRIPSYON KONDISYON FIZIK AK SANTIMAN II

move	**1**	angry/mad	enkyete	**10**	worried
debòde/ dechennen	**2**	furious	pè/lapè	**11**	scared/ afraid
degoute	**3**	disgusted	anbete	**12**	bored
fache	**4**	frustrated	fyè	**13**	proud
sezi	**5**	surprised	jennen	**14**	embarrassed
choke	**6**	shocked	jalou	**15**	jealous
sèl	**7**	lonely	bwouye	**16**	confused
nostaljik	**8**	homesick			
annève	**9**	nervous			

A. Are you **angry**?
B. Yes. I'm VERY **angry**.

What makes you angry?   What makes you nervous?   Do you ever feel embarrassed? When?

FRUITS

FWI

pòm **1** apple	kokoye **13** coconut	rezen **24** grapes
pèch **2** peach	zaboka **14** avocado	seriz **25** cherries
pwa **3** pear	kantaloup **15** cantaloupe	prin seche **26** prunes
fig **4** banana	melon myèl **16** honeydew (melon)	dat **27** dates
bannann **5** plantain		rezen sèk **28** raisins
prin **6** plum	melon dlo **17** watermelon	nwa **29** nuts
zabriko **7** apricot	zannanna **18** pineapple	franbwaz **30** raspberries
nektarin **8** nectarine	chadèk **19** grapefruit	blouberi **31** blueberries
kiwi **9** kiwi	sitwon jòn **20** lemon	frèz **32** strawberries
papay **10** papaya	sitwon vèt **21** lime	
mango **11** mango	zoranj **22** orange	
fig frans **12** fig	mandarin **23** tangerine	

[1–23]
A. This **apple** is delicious!
B. I'm glad you like it.

[24–32]
A. These **grapes** are delicious!
B. I'm glad you like them.

A. I'm hungry. Do we have any fruit?
B. Yes. We have _____s* and _____s.*

* With 15–19, use: We have _____ and _____.

A. Do we have any more _____s?†
B. No. I'll get some more when I go to the supermarket.

† With 15–19, use:
 Do we have any more _____?

What are your favorite fruits?
Which fruits don't you like?

Which of these fruits grow where you live?

Name and describe other fruits you know.

VEGETABLES

LEGIM

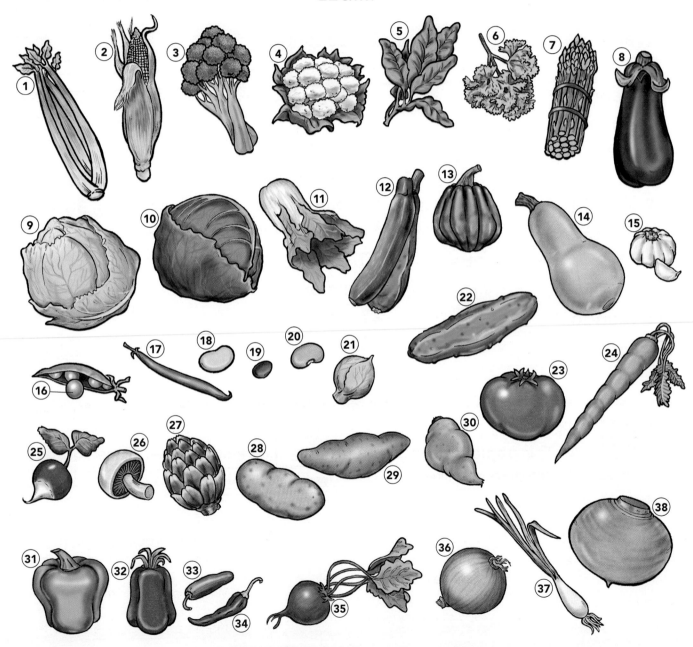

seleri	**1**	celery	lay	**15**	garlic	pòmtè	**28**	potato

seleri **1** celery
mayi **2** corn
bwokoli **3** broccoli
chouflè **4** cauliflower
zepina **5** spinach
pèsi **6** parsley
aspèj **7** asparagus
obèjin/ **8** eggplant
berejenn
leti **9** lettuce
chou **10** cabbage
bòk chòy **11** bok choy
eskwach **12** zucchini
jouwoumou **13** acorn
squash
jouwoumou **14** butternut
po jòn squash

lay **15** garlic
pwa nwa **16** pea
pwatann **17** string bean/
green bean
pwadsouch **18** lima bean
pwa nwa **19** black bean
pwa enkòni **20** kidney
bean
chou briksèl **21** brussels
sprout
konkonm **22** cucumber
tomat **23** tomato
kawòt **24** carrot
radi **25** radish
djondjon/ **26** mushroom
chanpiyon
aticho **27** artichoke

pòmtè **28** potato
patat **29** sweet
potato
patat jòn/yanm **30** yam
piman dous vèt **31** green pepper/
sweet pepper
piman dous **32** red pepper
wouj
piman zwazo **33** jalapeño
vèt (pepper)
piman zwazo **34** chili pepper
wouj
bètwouj **35** beet
zonyon **36** onion
siv **37** scallion/
green onion
nave **38** turnip

A. What do we need from the supermarket?
B. We need **celery*** and **pea**s.†

* 1–15   † 16–38

A. How do you like the
   __[1–15]__ ?
B. It's delicious.

A. How do you like the
   __[16–38]__ s?
B. They're delicious.

Which vegetables do you like?
Which vegetables don't you like?

Which of these vegetables grow where you live?

Name and describe other vegetables you know.

MEAT, POULTRY, AND SEAFOOD

VYANN, VOLAY AK MANJE LANMÈ

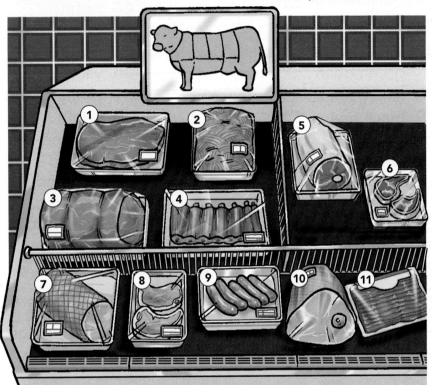

Vyann	**Meat**
biftèk	**1** steak
vyann moulen	**2** ground beef
wozbif/vyann bèf woti	**3** roast beef
kòt	**4** ribs
janm mouton	**5** leg of lamb
kotlèt mouton	**6** lamb chops
kochon	**7** pork
kotlèt kochon	**8** pork chops
sosis	**9** sausages
janbon	**10** ham
bekonn	**11** bacon

Volay	**Poultry**
poul	**12** chicken
blan poul	**13** chicken breasts
pye poul/ kwis poul	**14** chicken legs/ drumsticks
zèl poul	**15** chicken wings
kwis poul	**16** chicken thighs
kodenn	**17** turkey
kanna	**18** duck

Manje Lanmè Seafood

PWASON FISH

somon	**19** salmon
fletan	**20** halibut

pwason èglefen	**21** haddock
kalè	**22** flounder
twit	**23** trout
pwason	**24** catfish
file pwason	**25** filet of
bale	sole

PWASON NAN KOKI SHELLFISH

chèvrèt	**26** shrimp
koki senjak	**27** scallops
paloud	**28** clams
krab	**29** crabs
wonma	**30** lobster

[1–11]
A. Excuse me. Where can I find **steak**?
B. Look in the Meat Section.
A. Thank you.

[1–3, 5, 7, 10–12, 17–25, 30]
A. This _____ looks very fresh!
B. Let's get some for dinner.

[12–18]
A. Excuse me. Where can I find **chicken**?
B. Look in the Poultry Section.
A. Thank you.

[4, 6, 8, 9, 13–16, 26–29]
A. These _____ look very fresh!
B. Let's get some for dinner.

[19–30]
A. Excuse me. Where can I find **salmon**?
B. Look in the Seafood Section.
A. Thank you.

Do you eat meat, poultry, or seafood?
Which of these foods do you like?

Which of these foods are popular in your country?

PWODUI LÈT, JI AK BWASON

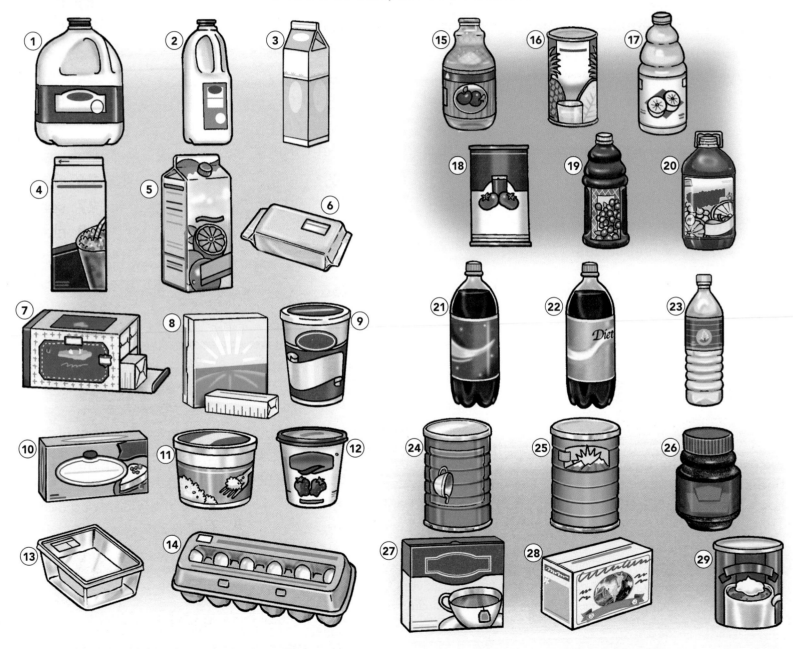

Pwodui lèt	Dairy Products		Ji	Juices		Kafe ak te	Coffee and Tea
lèt	**1** milk		ji pòm	**15** apple juice		kafe	**24** coffee
lèt degrese	**2** low-fat milk		ji zannanna	**16** pineapple juice		kafe	**25** decaffeinated
ti lèt	**3** skim milk		ji chadèk	**17** grapefruit juice		dekafeyine/	coffee/decaf
chokola ak lèt	**4** chocolate milk					kafe san kafeyin	
ji zoranj*	**5** orange juice*		ji tomat	**18** tomato juice		kafe	**26** instant
fwomaj	**6** cheese		ji rezen	**19** grape juice		enstantane	coffee
bè	**7** butter		ponch fwi	**20** fruit punch			
magarin/bè	**8** margarine					te	**27** tea
lèt si	**9** sour cream		**Bwason**	**Beverages**		te fèy	**28** herbal tea
krèm fwomaj	**10** cream cheese		soda	**21** soda		chokola/ chokola	**29** cocoa/ hot chocolate
lèt kaye	**11** cottage cheese		soda dyèt	**22** diet soda		an poud	mix
yogout	**12** yogurt		boutèy dlo	**23** bottled water			
tofou*	**13** tofu*						
ze	**14** eggs						

* Ji zoranj ak tofou pa gen lèt nan yo, men generalman, se nan seksyon sa w ap twouve yo.

A. I'm going to the supermarket to get some **milk**.
   Do we need anything else?
B. Yes. Please get some **apple juice**.

A. Excuse me. Where can I find _____?
B. Look in the _____ Section.
A. Thanks.

A. Look! _____ is on sale this week!
B. Let's get some!

* With 14, use: _____ are on sale this week.

Which of these foods do you like?

Which of these foods are good for you?

Which brands of these foods do you buy?

CHAKITRI, MANJE GLASE AK FRIDÒDÒY

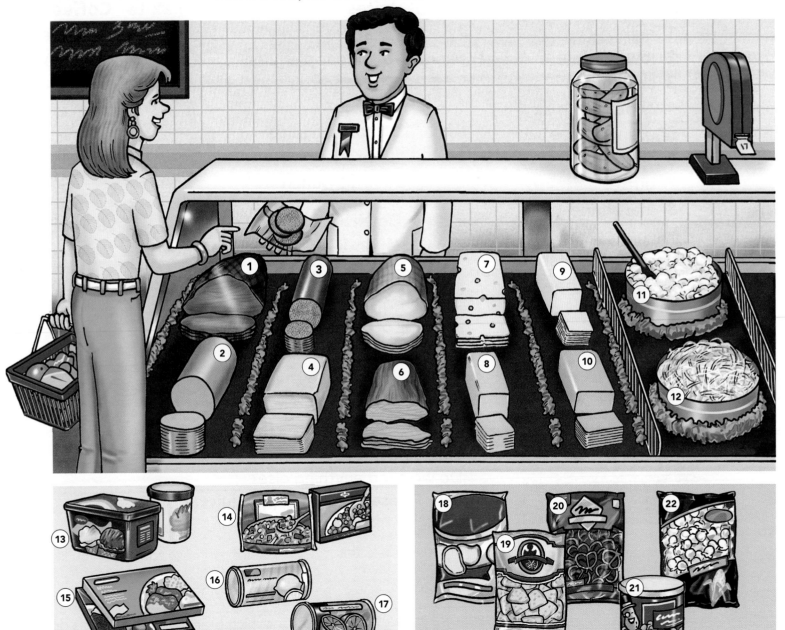

Chakitri		Deli
wozbif/vyann		
bèf woti	**1**	roast beef
mòtadèl	**2**	bologna
salami	**3**	salami
janbon	**4**	ham
kodenn	**5**	turkey
kònbif	**6**	corned beef
fwonmaj swis	**7**	Swiss cheese
fwonmaj ameriken	**8**	American cheese
mozarèl	**9**	mozzarella
fwonmaj cheda	**10**	cheddar cheese
salad ponmtè	**11**	potato salad
kòlslo	**12**	cole slaw

Manje glase		Frozen Foods
krèmalaglas/krèm	**13**	ice cream
legim konjile/glase	**14**	frozen vegetables
dine konjile/glase	**15**	frozen dinners
ji sitwon konjile/ glase/limonnad	**16**	frozen lemonade
ji zoranj konjile/glase	**17**	frozen orange juice

Fridòdòy		Snack Foods
pòmdetè fri	**18**	potato chips
tòtiya fri	**19**	tortilla chips
pretzel	**20**	pretzels
nwa	**21**	nuts
pòpkon	**22**	popcorn

A. Should we get some **roast beef**?
B. Good idea. And let's get some **potato salad**.

[1–12]
A. May I help you?
B. Yes, please. I'd like some _____.

[1–22]
A. Excuse me. Where is/are _____?
B. It's/They're in the _____ Section.

Which of these foods do you like?

Which brands of these foods do you buy?

EPISRI

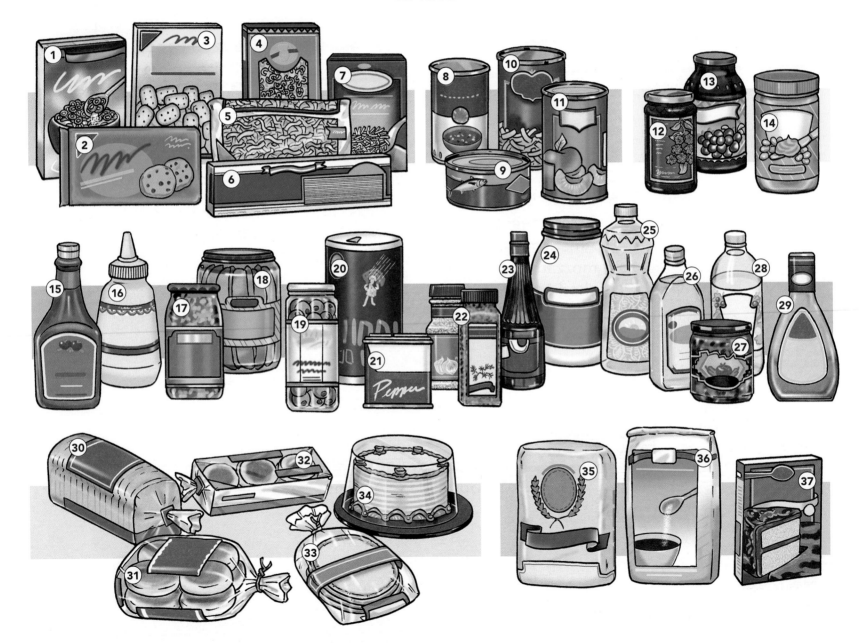

Pwovizyon Alimantè	Packaged Goods
sereyal	**1** cereal
bonbon	**2** cookies
biswit soda	**3** crackers
makawonni	**4** macaroni
makawonni plat	**5** noodles
espageti	**6** spaghetti
diri	**7** rice

Manje nan fèblan	Canned Goods
soup	**8** soup
touna	**9** tuna (fish)
legim nan fèblan	**10** (canned) vegetables
fwi nan fèblan	**11** (canned) fruit

Konfiti ak Jele	Jams and Jellies
konfiti	**12** jam
jele	**13** jelly
manba	**14** peanut butter

Asezonnay	Condiments
sòs tomat	**15** ketchup
moutad	**16** mustard
relich	**17** relish
pikliz	**18** pickles
oliv	**19** olives
sèl	**20** salt
pwav	**21** pepper
epis	**22** spices
sòs soya	**23** soy sauce
mayonnèz	**24** mayonnaise
luil/lwil (pou fè manje)	**25** (cooking) oil
luil/lwil oliv	**26** olive oil
salsa	**27** salsa
vinèg	**28** vinegar
sòs salad	**29** salad dressing

Manje nan fou	Baked Goods
pen	**30** bread
ti pen/pen won	**31** rolls
mèfin angle	**32** English muffins
pen pita	**33** pita bread
gato	**34** cake

Founiti pou Gato	Baking Products
farin	**35** flour
sik	**36** sugar
gato an poud	**37** cake mix

A. I got **cereal** and **soup**. What else is on the shopping list?
B. **Ketchup** and **bread**.

A. Excuse me. I'm looking for _____.
B. It's/They're next to the _____.

A. Pardon me. I'm looking for _____.
B. It's/They're between the _____ and the _____.

Which of these foods do you like?

Which brands of these foods do you buy?

PWODUI POU KAY, PWODUI BEBE AK MANJE BÈT KAY

Pwodui an papye — Paper Products

sèvyèt papye	1	napkins
gode papye	2	paper cups
mouchwa papye	3	tissues
chalimo	4	straws
asyèt papye	5	paper plates
tòchon papye	6	paper towels
ijyenik	7	toilet paper

Pwodui pou kay — Household Items

sache sandwich	8	sandwich bags
sak pou fatra	9	trash bags
savon	10	soap
savon likid	11	liquid soap
papye aliminyòm	12	aluminum foil
papye plastik	13	plastic wrap
pou vlope/papye sire	14	waxed paper

Pwodui Bebe — Baby Products

sereyal bebe	15	baby cereal
manje bebe	16	baby food
lèt bebe	17	formula
netwayèt bebe	18	wipes
kouchèt papye	19	(disposable) diapers

Manje Bèt Kay — Pet Food

manje chat	20	cat food
manje chyen	21	dog food

A. Excuse me. Where can I find **napkins**?
B. **Napkins**? Look in Aisle 4.

[7, 10–17, 20, 21]
A. We forgot to get _____!
B. I'll get it. Where is it?
A. It's in Aisle _____.

[1–6, 8, 9, 18, 19]
A. We forgot to get _____!
B. I'll get them. Where are they?
A. They're in Aisle _____.

What do you need from the supermarket?
Make a complete shopping list!

THE SUPERMARKET

SIPÈMAKÈT LA

ale/zèl	**1**	aisle	liy esprès	**12**	express checkout (line)
kliyan	**2**	shopper/customer	eskanè	**13**	scanner
panyen makèt	**3**	shopping basket	sache plastik	**14**	plastic bag
liy kès	**4**	checkout line	dirijè/manadjè	**15**	manager
kontwa kès	**5**	checkout counter	kesye	**16**	clerk
kès otomatik	**6**	cash register	balans	**17**	scale
charyo	**7**	shopping cart	machin pou remèt fèblan	**18**	can-return machine
koupon	**8**	coupons	machin pou remèt boutèy	**19**	bottle-return machine
kesye	**9**	cashier			
sache papye	**10**	paper bag			
anbalè	**11**	bagger/packer			

A. This is a gigantic supermarket!
B. It is! Look at all the **aisle**s!

Where do you usually shop for food? Do you go to a supermarket, or do you go to a small grocery store? Describe the place where you shop.

Describe the differences between U.S. supermarkets and food stores in your country.

RESIPYAN AK KANTITE

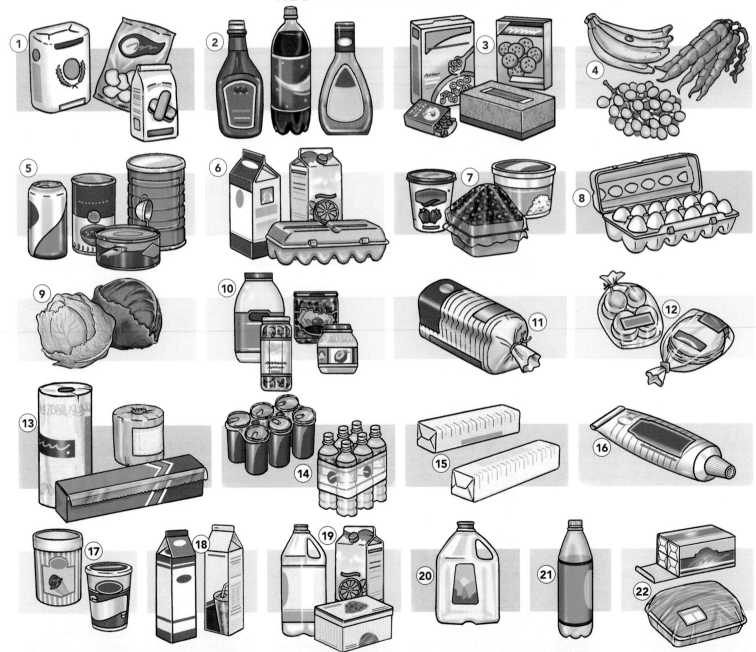

sak/sache	**1** bag	bokal	**10** jar	demi-galon	**19** half-gallon
boutèy	**2** bottle	pen tranche	**11** loaf/loaves	galon	**20** gallon
bwat	**3** box	anbalaj	**12** package	lit	**21** liter
pat/pake/grap	**4** bunch	woulo	**13** roll	liv	**22** pound
bwat fèblan	**5** can	pake sis/sikspak	**14** six-pack		
katon	**6** carton	baton	**15** stick		
bwat	**7** container	tib	**16** tube		
douzèn	**8** dozen*	pent	**17** pint		
tèt	**9** head	ka	**18** quart		

* "a dozen eggs," PA "a dozen of eggs"

A. Please get a **bag** of *flour* when you go to the supermarket.
B. A **bag** of *flour*? Okay.

A. Please get two **bottles** of *ketchup* when you go to the supermarket.
B. Two **bottles** of *ketchup*? Okay.

[At home]
A. What did you get at the supermarket?
B. I got ____, ____, and ____.

[In a supermarket]
A. This is the express checkout line. Do you have more than eight items?
B. No. I only have ____, ____, and ____.

Open your kitchen cabinets and refrigerator. Make a list of all the things you find.

What do you do with empty bottles, jars, and cans? Do you recycle them, reuse them, or throw them away?

PWA AK MEZI I

 kiyè kafe **teaspoon**
tsp.

 kiyè tab **tablespoon**
Tbsp.

 yon ons likid **1 (fluid) ounce**
1 ons likid **1 fl. oz.**

 tas **cup**
c.
8 ons likid **8 fl. ozs.**

 pent **pint**
pt.
16 ons likid **16 fl. ozs.**

 ka **quart**
qt.
32 ons likid **32 fl. ozs.**

 galon **gallon**
gal.
128 ons likid **128 fl. ozs.**

A. How much water should I put in?
B. The recipe says to add one _____ of water.

A. This fruit punch is delicious! What's in it?
B. Two _____s of apple juice, three _____
of orange juice, and a _____ of grape juice.

yon ons   an ounce

1 ons.   oz.

yon ka liiv   a quarter
              of a pound

1/4 liv   1/4 lb.
4 ons.   4 ozs.

demi   half a
liv   pound

1/2 liv   1/2 lb.
8 ons.   8 ozs.

twaka   three-
liv   quarters
        of a pound

3/4 liv   3/4 lb.
12 ons.   12 ozs.

yon liv   a pound

1 liv   lb.
16 ons.   16 ozs.

A. How much roast beef would you like?
B. I'd like _____, please.
A. Anything else?
B. Yes. Please give me _____ of Swiss cheese.

A. This chili tastes very good! What did you put
in it?
B. _____ of ground beef, _____ of beans, _____ of
tomatoes, and _____ of chili powder.

PREPARASYON AK RESÈT POU KWIT MANJE

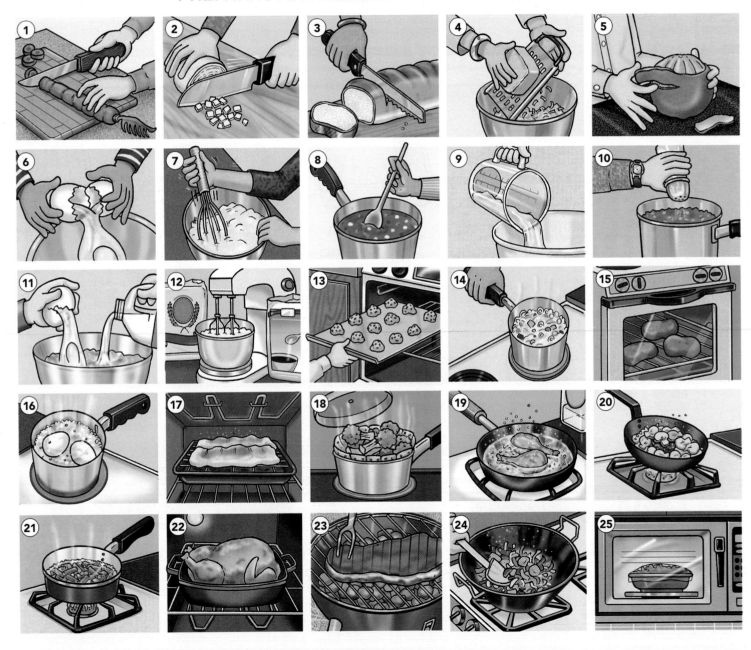

koupe	**1** cut (up)		kwit	**14** cook
rache	**2** chop (up)		anfounen	**15** bake
tranche	**3** slice		bouyi	**16** boil
graje	**4** grate		griye	**17** broil
kale	**5** peel		kwit nan vapè	**18** steam
kase	**6** break		fri	**19** fry
bat	**7** beat		frikase/sote	**20** saute
brase	**8** stir		toufe	**21** simmer
vide	**9** pour		griye	**22** roast
ajoute	**10** add		recho griyad	**23** barbecue / grill
mete ansanm ___ ak ___	**11** combine ___ and ___		fritay brase	**24** stir-fry
melanje ___ ak ___	**12** mix ___ and ___		mikwowev	**25** microwave
mete ___ nan ___	**13** put ___ in ___			

A. Can I help you?
B. Yes. Please **cut up** the vegetables.

[1–25]
A. What are you doing?
B. I'm _____ing the ....

[14–25]
A. How long should I _____ the ....?
B. _____ the .... for .... minutes / seconds.

What's your favorite recipe? Give instructions and use the units of measure on pages 114 and 115. For example:

Mix a cup of flour and two tablespoons of sugar.
Add half a pound of butter.
Bake at 350° (degrees) for twenty minutes.

FAST FOOD

MANJE PRESE

anmbègè	**1**	hamburger	krèm	**14**	ice cream
chizbègè	**2**	cheeseburger	yogout konjile/glase	**15**	frozen yogurt
òtdòg	**3**	hot dog	lèt ak krèm/melkchek	**16**	milkshake
sandwich pwason	**4**	fish sandwich	soda	**17**	soda
sandwich poul	**5**	chicken sandwich	kouvèti	**18**	lids
poul fri	**6**	fried chicken	gode papye	**19**	paper cups
ponmtè fri	**7**	french fries	chalimo	**20**	straws
nachos	**8**	nachos	sèvyèt papye	**21**	napkins
tako	**9**	taco	fouchèt ak kouto plastik	**22**	plastic utensils
bourito	**10**	burrito	sòs tomat	**23**	ketchup
tranch pitza	**11**	slice of pizza	moutad	**24**	mustard
bòl chili	**12**	bowl of chili	mayonnèz	**25**	mayonnaise
salad	**13**	salad	relich	**26**	relish
			sòs salad	**27**	salad dressing

A. May I help you?
B. Yes. I'd like a/an ___[1–5, 9–17]___ / an order of ___[6–8]___ .

A. Excuse me. We're almost out of ___[18–27]___ .
B. I'll get some more from the supply room. Thanks for telling me.

Do you go to fast-food restaurants? Which ones? How often? What do you order?

Are there fast-food restaurants in your country? Are they popular? What foods do they have?

MAGAZEN POU MANJE LEJÈ AK SANDWICH

dounòt	**1**	donut		te glase	**16**	iced tea
ponmkèt	**2**	muffin		limonnad	**17**	lemonade
begèl	**3**	bagel		chokola cho	**18**	hot chocolate
patistri	**4**	danish/pastry		lèt	**19**	milk
biswit	**5**	biscuit		sandwich pwason	**20**	tuna fish
kwasan	**6**	croissant		touna		sandwich
ze	**7**	eggs		sandwich	**21**	egg salad
pannkek	**8**	pancakes		salad ze		sandwich
wafal	**9**	waffles		sandwich	**22**	chicken salad
pen griye	**10**	toast		salad poul		sandwich
la	**11**	bacon		sandwich janbon	**23**	ham and cheese
sosis	**12**	sausages		ak fwomaj		sandwich
kafe	**13**	coffee		BLT/sandwich	**24**	BLT/bacon,
kafe dekafeyine	**14**	decaf coffee		bekonn, leti		lettuce,
te	**15**	tea		ak tomat		and tomato
						sandwich

A. May I help you?
B. Yes. I'd like a ___[1–6]___ /an order of ___[7–12]___ , please.
A. Anything to drink?
B. Yes. I'll have a small/medium-size/large/
extra-large ___[13–19]___ .

A. I'd like a ___[20–24]___ , please.
B. What do you want on it?
A. Lettuce/tomato/mayonnaise/mustard/. . .

Do you like these foods? Which ones? Where do you get them? How often do you have them?

RESTORAN AN I

mete kliyan yo chita	**A**	seat the customers
vide dlo a	**B**	pour the water
pran kòmann lan	**C**	take the order
sèvi manje a	**D**	serve the meal

otès	**1**	hostess
obèjis	**2**	host
kliyan	**3**	diner / customer
konpatiman	**4**	booth
tab	**5**	table
chèz wo pou bebe	**6**	high chair
chèz pou wose bebe	**7**	booster seat

meni	**8**	menu
panyen pen	**9**	bread basket
moun ki ranmase asyèt	**10**	busperson
madmwazèl / sèvant	**11**	waitress / server
gason / sèvant	**12**	waiter / server
bifè salad	**13**	salad bar
kote pou manje	**14**	dining room
kwizin	**15**	kitchen
kizinye	**16**	chef

[A–D]
A. Please **seat the customers**.
B. All right. I'll **seat the customers** right away.

[1, 2, 10–12, 16]
A. Do you have any job openings?
B. Yes. We're looking for a **hostess**.

[4–9]
A. Would you like a **booth**?
B. Yes, please.

[13–16]
A. This restaurant has a wonderful **salad bar**.
B. I agree.

Tell about a restaurant you know. Describe the place and the people. (Is the restaurant large or small? How many tables are there? How many people work there? Is there a salad bar? . . .)

RESTORAN AN II

netwaye tab la	**A** clear the table	plat salad	**7** salad plate	**ajantri**	**silverware**
peye chèk la	**B** pay the check	plat pen ak bè	**8** bread-and-butter plate	fouchèt salad	**16** salad fork
kite tep	**C** leave a tip	asyèt manje aswè	**9** dinner plate	fouchèt pou manje aswè	**17** dinner fork
ranje tab la	**D** set the table	bòl soup	**10** soup bowl	kouto	**18** knife
chanm pou asyèt	**1** dishroom	vè pou dlo	**11** water glass	ti kiyè	**19** teaspoon
machin vesèl	**2** dishwasher	vè pou diven	**12** wine glass	kiyè soup	**20** soup spoon
plato	**3** tray	tas	**13** cup	kouto bè	**21** butter knife
charèt desè	**4** dessert cart	soukoup	**14** saucer		
bòdwo	**5** check	sèvyèt papye	**15** napkin		
tep/poubwa/ kichòy	**6** tip				

[A–D]

A. Please **clear the table**.
B. All right. I'll **clear the table** right away.

[7–21]

A. Excuse me. Where does the **salad fork** go?
B. It goes *to the left of* the **dinner fork**.

A. Excuse me. Where does the **bread-and-butter plate** go?
B. It goes *to the right of* the **salad plate**.

A. Excuse me. Where does the **cup** go?
B. It goes *on* the **saucer**.

A. Excuse me. Where does the **teaspoon** go?
B. It goes *between* the **knife** and the **soup spoon**.

Practice giving directions. Tell someone how to set a table. (Put the . . . . . .)

A RESTAURANT MENU

MENI RESTORAN AN

tas fwi	**1** fruit cup
ji tomat	**2** tomato juice
koktèl kribich	**3** shrimp cocktail
zèl poul	**4** chicken wings
nachos	**5** nachos
po ponmtè	**6** potato skins
salad vèt	**7** tossed salad
salad grèk	**8** Greek salad
salad zepina	**9** spinach salad
antipasto	**10** antipasto (plate)
salad Seza	**11** Caesar salad

vyann moulen	**12** meatloaf
vyann bèf	**13** roast beef
poul nan fou	**14** baked chicken
pwason bouyi	**15** broiled fish
vèmisèl ak boulèt	**16** spaghetti and meatballs
kòtlèt vo	**17** veal cutlet
pòmtè lan fou	**18** a baked potato
pire pòmtè	**19** mashed potatoes
pòmtè fri	**20** french fries
diri	**21** rice
vèmisèl	**22** noodles
legim melanje	**23** mixed vegetables

gato chokola	**24** chocolate cake
tat pòm	**25** apple pie
krèmalaglas	**26** ice cream
jelo	**27** jello
poudin	**28** pudding
sonnde	**29** ice cream sundae

[Ordering dinner]

A. May I take your order?
B. Yes, please. For the appetizer, I'd like the ___[1–6]___.
A. And what kind of salad would you like?
B. I'll have the ___[7–11]___.
A. And for the main course?
B. I'd like the ___[12–17]___, please.
A. What side dish would you like with that?
B. Hmm. I think I'll have ___[18–23]___.

[Ordering dessert]

A. Would you like some dessert?
B. Yes. I'll have ___[24–28]___ /an ___[29]___.

Tell about the food at a restaurant you know.
What's on the menu?

What are some typical foods on the menus of
restaurants in your country?

COLORS

KOULÈ

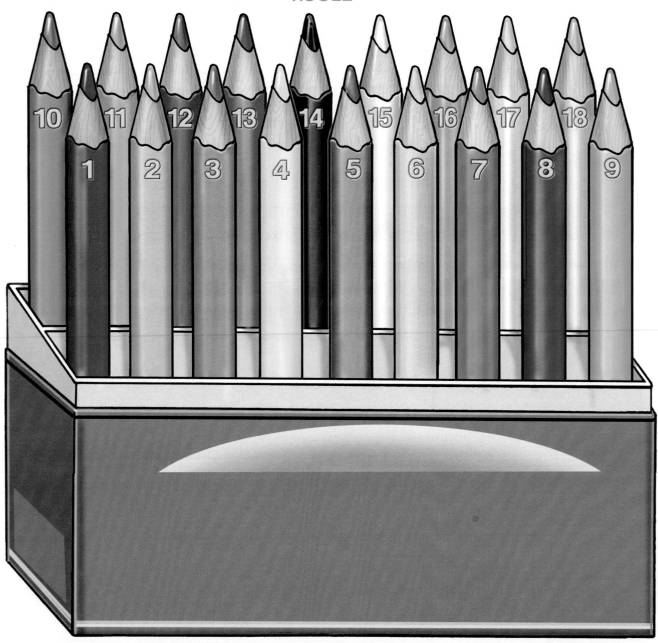

wouj	**1**	red	vèt	**10**	green
wòz	**2**	pink	vèt pal	**11**	light green
jòn oranji	**3**	orange	vèt fonse	**12**	dark green
jòn	**4**	yellow	mòv/vyolet	**13**	purple
mawon	**5**	brown	nwa	**14**	black
bèj	**6**	beige	blan	**15**	white
ble	**7**	blue	gri	**16**	gray
ble maren	**8**	navy blue	ajan	**17**	silver
tikwaz	**9**	turquoise	lò	**18**	gold

A. What's your favorite color?
B. **Red**.

A. I like your _____ shirt.
You look very good in _____.
B. Thank you. _____ is my
favorite color.

A. My TV is broken.
B. What's the matter with it?
A. People's faces are _____,
the sky is _____, and the
grass is _____!

Do you know the flags of different countries?
What are the colors of flags you know?

What color makes you happy? What color
makes you sad? Why?

RAD

kòsaj	**1**	blouse	inifòm	**15**	uniform
jip	**2**	skirt	chemizèt ak manch	**16**	T-shirt
chemiz	**3**	shirt	pantalon kout	**17**	shorts
pantalon	**4**	pants/slacks	rad gwosès	**18**	maternity dress
chemiz espò	**5**	sport shirt	rad yon pyès	**19**	jumpsuit
djin	**6**	jeans	jile	**20**	vest
mayo	**7**	knit shirt/jersey	rad toudinpyès	**21**	jumper
wòb	**8**	dress	rad/tounik/kazak	**22**	tunic
chanday	**9**	sweater	kolan	**23**	leggings
levit	**10**	jacket	salopèt	**24**	overalls
manto espò/ vès espò	**11**	sport coat/ sport jacket	kòl wo	**25**	turtleneck
kostim	**12**	suit	esmokin	**26**	tuxedo
kostim twa pyès	**13**	three-piece suit	wozèt	**27**	bow tie
kravat	**14**	tie	wòb long	**28**	(evening) gown

A. I think I'll wear my new **blouse** today.
B. Good idea!

A. I really like your _____.
B. Thank you.
A. Where did you get it/them?
B. At ....

A. Oh, no! I just ripped my _____!
B. What a shame!

What clothing items in this lesson do you wear?

What color clothing do you like to wear?

What do you wear at work or at school? at parties? at weddings?

OUTERWEAR

RAD POU FREDI

manto	**1**	coat	parapli	**15**	umbrella
manto	**2**	overcoat	poncho	**16**	poncho
chapo	**3**	hat	jakèt lapli	**17**	rain jacket
blouzon	**4**	jacket	bòt lapli	**18**	rain boots
echap	**5**	scarf	chapo eski	**19**	ski hat
vès chanday	**6**	sweater jacket	jakèt eski	**20**	ski jacket
kolan	**7**	tights	gan	**21**	gloves
kaskèt	**8**	cap	mask eski	**22**	ski mask
vès kui	**9**	leather jacket	jakèt kapitonnen	**23**	down jacket
kaskèt bisbòl	**10**	baseball cap	gan sandwèt	**24**	mittens
parabriz	**11**	windbreaker	manto eskimo	**25**	parka
padsi	**12**	raincoat	linèt solèy	**26**	sunglasses
chapo pou lapli	**13**	rain hat	pwotèj zorèy	**27**	ear muffs
padsi kwaze	**14**	trench coat	jile kapitonnen	**28**	down vest

A. What's the weather like today?
B. It's cool/cold/raining/snowing.
A. I think I'll wear my _____.

[1–6, 8–17, 19, 20, 22, 23, 25, 28]
A. May I help you?
B. Yes, please. I'm looking for a/an _____.

[7, 18, 21, 24, 26, 27]
A. May I help you?
B. Yes, please. I'm looking for _____.

What do you wear outside when the weather is cool?/when it's raining?/when it's very cold?

SLEEPWEAR AND UNDERWEAR

RAD POU DÒMI AK SOUVÈTMAN

pijama	**1**	pajamas		chosèt	**12**	socks
chemizdennwit long	**2**	nightgown		kilòt	**13**	panties
chemizdennwit kout	**3**	nightshirt		slip/kilòt	**14**	briefs / underpants
wòbdechanm	**4**	bathrobe				
pantouf	**5**	slippers		soutyen	**15**	bra
kostim triko / kostim lenn	**6**	blanket sleeper		kamizòl	**16**	camisole
				jipon	**17**	slip
chemizèt	**7**	undershirt		ba	**18**	stockings
jòki/slip	**8**	underpants		ba kilòt	**19**	pantyhose
kalson	**9**	boxer shorts		kolan	**20**	tights
sipò atletik / sispanswa	**10**	athletic supporter / jockstrap		ba/chosèt long	**21**	knee socks
kalson long	**11**	long underwear				

A. I can't find my new _____.
B. Did you look in the bureau / dresser / closet?
A. Yes, I did.
B. Then it's / they're probably in the wash.

What sleepwear items do you wear? What sleepwear items do people in your family wear?

RAD POU FÈ EGZÈSIS AK SOULYE

chemizèt san manch	**1**	tank top
chòt espò/ chòt pou kouri	**2**	running shorts
bando espò	**3**	sweatband
kostim espò	**4**	jogging suit
chemizèt ak manch	**5**	T-shirt
kolan espò	**6**	lycra shorts/ bike shorts
chemizèt espò	**7**	sweatshirt
pantalon espò	**8**	sweatpants
rad kouvri kostimdeben	**9**	cover-up
kostimdeben	**10**	swimsuit/ bathing suit

chòt	**11**	swimming trunks/ swimsuit/ bathing suit
leyota	**12**	leotard
soulye	**13**	shoes
talon kikit	**14**	(high) heels
tennis	**15**	sneakers
soulye tenis	**16**	tennis shoes
soulye kous	**17**	running shoes
bòt tenis	**18**	high-tops/ high-top sneakers
sandal	**19**	sandals
sapat	**20**	thongs/flip-flops
bòt	**21**	boots
bòt pou travay	**22**	work boots

[1–12]
A. Excuse me. I found this/these _____ in the dryer. Is it/Are they yours?
B. Yes. It's/They're mine. Thank you.

[13–22]
A. Are those new _____?
B. Yes, they are.
A. They're very nice.
B. Thanks.

Do you exercise? What do you do? What kind of clothing do you wear when you exercise?

What kind of shoes do you wear when you go to work or to school? when you exercise? when you relax at home? when you go out with friends or family members?

BIJOU AK AKSESWA

bag	**1**	ring
bag fiyansay	**2**	engagement ring
alyans	**3**	wedding ring/ wedding band
zanno	**4**	earrings
kolye	**5**	necklace
kolye pèl	**6**	pearl necklace/ pearls
chenn	**7**	chain
krizokal	**8**	beads
bròch	**9**	pin
medalyon	**10**	locket
brasle	**11**	bracelet
barèt	**12**	barrette
bouton manch	**13**	cuff links

bretèl	**14**	suspenders
mont	**15**	watch
mouchwa	**16**	handkerchief
pòt kle	**17**	key ring
ti bous	**18**	change purse
pòtfèy	**19**	wallet
sentiwon	**20**	belt
bous/ sakamanch	**21**	purse/handbag/ pocketbook
valiz	**22**	shoulder bag
sakaliv/valiz liv	**23**	book bag
sakado/bakpak	**24**	backpack
valiz makiyaj	**25**	makeup bag
valiz/sakí	**26**	briefcase

A. Oh, no! I think I lost my **ring**!
B. I'll help you look for it.

A. Oh, no! I think I lost my **earrings**!
B. I'll help you look for them.

[In a store]
A. Excuse me. Is this/Are these _____ on sale this week?
B. Yes. It's/They're half price.

[On the street]
A. Help! Police! Stop that man/woman!
B. What happened?!
A. He/She just stole my _____ and my _____!

Do you like to wear jewelry? What jewelry do you have?

In your country, what do men, women, and children use to carry their things?

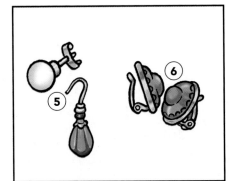

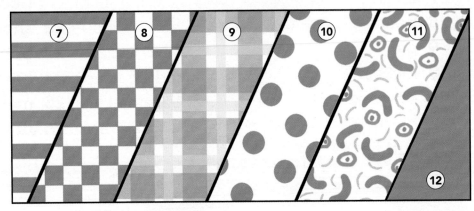

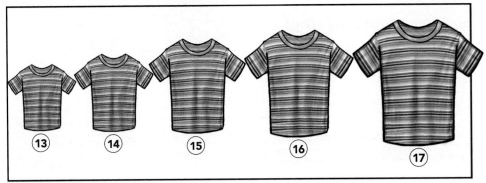

Kalite Rad	Types of Clothing
chemiz manch long	**1** long-sleeved shirt
chemiz manch kout	**2** short-sleeved shirt
chemiz san manch	**3** sleeveless shirt
(chanday) kòl wo	**4** turtleneck (shirt)
zanno pèse	**5** pierced earrings
zanno plake	**6** clip-on earrings

Desen	Patterns
ak ba	**7** striped
ak karo	**8** checked
twal ekosè	**9** plaid
rad ak boul	**10** polka-dotted
enprime	**11** print
ble ini	**12** solid *blue*

Mezi	Sizes
tou piti	**13** extra-small
piti	**14** small
medyòm/mwayèn	**15** medium
laj/gwo	**16** large
laj anpil	**17** extra-large

[1–4]
A. May I help you?
B. Yes, please. I'm looking for a *shirt*.
A. What kind?
B. I'm looking for a *long-sleeved shirt*.

[7–12]
A. How do you like this _____ tie/shirt/skirt?
B. Actually, I prefer that _____ one.

[13–17]
A. What size are you looking for?
B. _____.

Describe your favorite clothing items. For each item, tell about the color, the size, and the pattern.

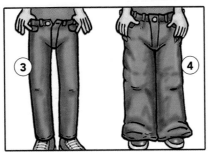

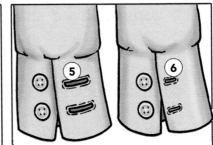

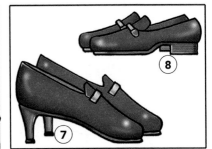

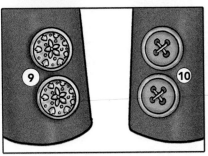

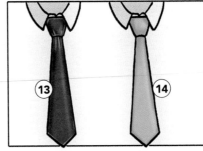

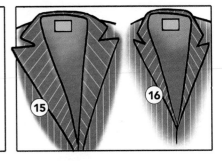

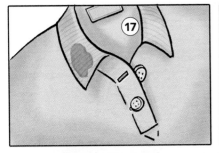

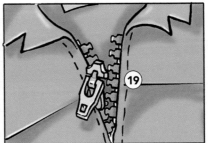

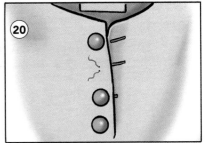

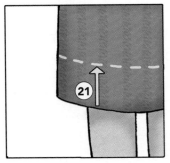

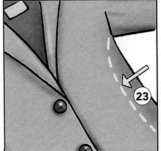

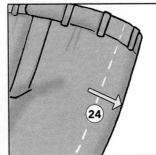

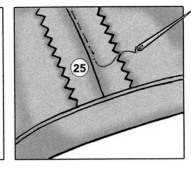

long – kout	**1–2** long – short	*kòlèt* tache	**17** stained *collar*
sere – bagi	**3–4** tight – loose/baggy	*pòch* chire	**18** ripped/torn *pocket*
laj/gwo – piti	**5–6** large/big – small	*zip* kase	**19** broken *zipper*
wo – ba	**7–8** high – low	*bouton* manke	**20** missing *button*
bòzò – senp	**9–10** fancy – plain	monte *jip la*	**21** shorten the *skirt*
lou – leje	**11–12** heavy – light	lonje *manch yo*	**22** lengthen the *sleeves*
fonse – klè	**13–14** dark – light	fèmen *jile a*	**23** take in the *jacket*
laj – etwat	**15–16** wide – narrow	laji *pantalon an*	**24** let out the *pants*
		ranje/repare *kouti a*	**25** fix/repair the *seam*

[1–2]
A. Are the sleeves too **long**?
B. No. They're too **short**.

1–2   Are the sleeves too _____?
3–4   Are the pants too _____?
5–6   Are the buttonholes too _____?
7–8   Are the heels too _____?

9–10   Are the buttons too _____?
11–12   Is the coat too _____?
13–14   Is the color too _____?
15–16   Are the lapels too _____?

[17–20]
A. What's the matter with it?
B. It has a **stained** *collar*.

[21–25]
A. Please **shorten** the *skirt*.
B. **Shorten** the *skirt*? Okay.

Tell about the differences between clothing people wear now and clothing people wore a long time ago.

THE DEPARTMENT STORE

MAGAZEN VARYETE

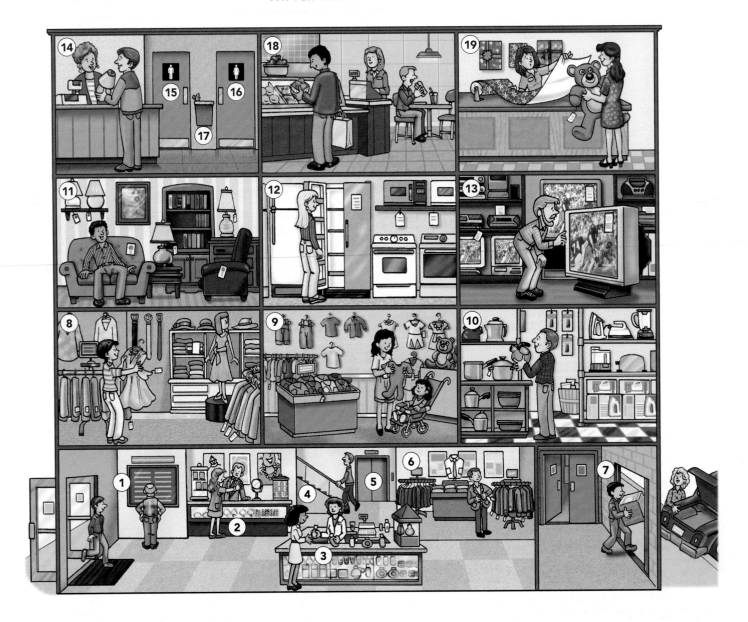

tablo enfòmasyon	**1** (store) directory	Depatman mèb	**11** Furniture Department
kontwa Bijou	**2** Jewelry Counter	Depatman aparèy menaje	**12** Household Appliances Department
kontwa Pafen	**3** Perfume Counter		
eskalye woulant	**4** escalator	Depatman elektwonik	**13** Electronics Department
asansè	**5** elevator		
Depatman rad gason	**6** Men's Clothing Department	kontwa Sèvis Kliyan	**14** Customer Service Counter
zòn livrezon machandiz	**7** customer pickup area	chanm gason	**15** men's room
		chanm fi	**16** ladies' room
Depatman rad fanm	**8** Women's Clothing Department	fontèn dlo	**17** water fountain
		magazen ti goute	**18** snack bar
Depatman rad timoun	**9** Children's Clothing Department	kontwa Papye Kado	**19** Gift Wrap Counter
Depatman bagay kay	**10** Housewares Department		

A. Excuse me. Where's the **store directory**?
B. It's over there, next to the **Jewelry Counter**.
A. Thanks.
B. You're welcome.

A. Excuse me. Do you sell *ties**?
B. Yes. You can find *ties** in the ___[6, 8–13]___ /at the __[2, 3]__ .
A. Thank you.

**ties/bracelets/dresses/toasters/. . .*

Describe a department store you know. Tell what is on each floor.

SHOPPING

AP ACHTE

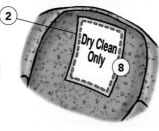

achte	**A** buy		rabè	**5**	discount
remèt	**B** return		mezi	**6**	size
chanje	**C** exchange		materyèl	**7**	material
eseye/mezire	**D** try on		enstriksyon pou	**8**	care
peye	**E** pay for		okipe rad		instructions
pran	**F** get some		pri nòmal	**9**	regular price
enfòmasyon	information about		pri pou vant	**10**	sale price
			pri	**11**	price
siy vant	**1** sale sign		taks sou lavant	**12**	sales tax
etikèt	**2** label		pri total	**13**	total price
etikèt pri	**3** price tag				
resi	**4** receipt				

A. May I help you?
B. Yes, please. I want to _____[A–F]_____ this item.
A. Certainly. I'll be glad to help you.

A. {What's the _____[5–7, 9–13]_____ ?
{What are the ___[8]___ ?
B. _____.
A. Are you sure?
B. Yes. Look at the ___[1–4]___ !

Which stores in your area have sales? How often?

Tell about something you bought on sale.

VIDEO, AUDIO, TELEPHONES, AND CAMERAS

VIDEYO, ODYO, TELEFÒN AK KAMERA

televizyon	**1**	TV/television	aparèy estereyo pòtab/ pèsonnèl	**17**	portable stereo system/boombox
DVD	**2**	DVD	aparèy CD pèsonnèl	**18**	personal CD player
aparèy DVD	**3**	DVD player	aparèy kasèt pòtatif	**19**	personal cassette player
videyo/kasèt videyo/ videyotep	**4**	video/ videotape	ekoutè	**20**	headphones
VCR	**5**	VCR	aparèy pòtab dijital pou tande	**21**	personal digital audio player
Kodak/kamera/ videyo	**6**	camcorder/ video camera	sistèm jwèt videyo	**22**	video game system
radyo	**7**	radio	jwèt videyo	**23**	video game
radyo revèy	**8**	clock radio	telefòn	**24**	telephone/phone
anrejistrè	**9**	tape recorder	telefòn selilè	**25**	cell phone
mikwo	**10**	microphone	repondè	**26**	answering machine
sistèm estereyo	**11**	stereo system/ sound system	kalkilatè	**27**	calculator
CD	**12**	CD	kamera (35milimèt)	**28**	(35 millimeter) camera
aparèy CD	**13**	CD player	vè	**29**	lens
odyo tep/kasèt	**14**	audiotape	film	**30**	film
kasètofòn	**15**	tape deck	kamera dijital	**31**	digital camera
wopalè	**16**	speakers	disk memwa	**32**	memory disk
			flach (atachman)	**33**	flash (attachment)

A. May I help you?
B. Yes, please. I'm looking for a **TV**.

With 16, 20, 30, use: I'm looking for _____.

A. Excuse me. Do you sell _____(s)?*
B. Yes. We have a large selection of _____s.

With 30, use: Do you sell _____?

A. I like your new _____.
   Where did you get it/them?
B. At ....
   (name of store)

What equipment in this lesson do you have or want?

In your opinion, which brands of equipment are the best?

KONPITÈ

Pyès Konpitè	**Computer Hardware**
konpitè	**1** (desktop) computer
CPU	**2** CPU/central processing unit
monitè/ekran	**3** monitor/screen
CD-ROM drive	**4** CD-ROM drive
CD-ROM	**5** CD-ROM
disk pwosesè	**6** disk drive
diskèt	**7** (floppy) disk
klavye	**8** keyboard
sourit	**9** mouse
monitè plat/ ekran LCD	**10** flat panel screen/ LCD screen
konpitè pòtab	**11** notebook computer

bwa pou dirije	**12** joystick
boul pou dirije	**13** track ball
modèm	**14** modem
pwoteksyon kont gwo voltaj	**15** surge protector
enprimant	**16** printer
eskanè/eskritè	**17** scanner
kab	**18** cable

Lojisyèl Konpitè	**Computer Software**
pwogram mo	**19** word-processing program
pwogram kontablite	**20** spreadsheet program
pwogram lojisyèl edikasyon	**21** educational software program
jwèt konpitè	**22** computer game

A. Can you recommend a good **computer**?
B. Yes. This **computer** here is excellent.

A. Is that a new _____?
B. Yes.
A. Where did you get it?
B. At ......*(name of store)*...... .

A. May I help you?
B. Yes, please. Do you sell _____s?
A. Yes. We carry a complete line of _____s.

Do you use a computer? When?

In your opinion, why are computers important?

BANK LAN

fè yon depo	**A** make a deposit	chèk pou vwayaje	**4** traveler's check
fè yon tiraj	**B** make a withdrawal	kanè labank	**5** bankbook
touché yon chèk	**C** cash a check	kat ATM	**6** ATM card
achte chèk	**D** get traveler's checks	kat kredi	**7** credit card
		kavo	**8** (bank) vault
ouvri yon kont	**E** open an account	bwat depo	**9** safe deposit box
aplike pou prete lajan	**F** apply for a loan	kesye	**10** teller
		ajan sekirite	**11** security guard
chanje lajan	**G** exchange currency	machin tiraj otoèmatik/machin ATM	**12** ATM (machine)/ cash machine
fich depo	**1** deposit slip		
fich tiraj	**2** withdrawal slip	ofisye labank	**13** bank officer
chèk	**3** check		

[A–G]

A. Where are you going?
B. I'm going to the bank.
   I have to _____.

[5–7]

A. What are you looking for?
B. My _____. I can't find it anywhere!

[8–13]

A. How many _____s does the State Street Bank have?
B. ....

Do you have a bank account? What kind? Where? What do you do at the bank?

Do you ever use traveler's checks? When?

Do you have a credit card? What kind? When do you use it?

FINANS

Jan pou Peye	Forms of Payment
lajan	**1** cash
chèk	**2** check
kat kredi	**3** credit card
monnenòdè	**4** money order
chèk vwayaj	**5** traveler's check

Bòdwo Kay	Household Bills
lwaye	**6** rent
pòtèk	**7** mortgage payment
bil/bòdwo elektrik	**8** electric bill
bil telefòn	**9** telephone bill
bil/bòdwo gaz	**10** gas bill
bil/bòdwo luil/chofaj	**11** oil bill/heating bill
bil/bòdwo dlo	**12** water bill
bil/bòdwo kab	**13** cable TV bill
peye machin nan	**14** car payment
bil/bòdwo kat kredi	**15** credit card bill

Finans Fanmi	Family Finances
balanse kannè chek la	**16** balance the checkbook
ekri yon chèk	**17** write a check
bank nan konpitè	**18** bank online
kannè chèk	**19** checkbook
fèy kontwòl chèk	**20** check register
eta kont pa mwa	**21** monthly statement

Sèvi ak machin ATM	Using an ATM Machine
mete kat ATM nan andedan	**22** insert the ATM card
mete nimewo PIN* nan	**23** enter your PIN* number
chwazi yon tranzaksyon	**24** select a transaction
fè yon depo	**25** make a deposit
pran/retire lajan	**26** withdraw/get cash
transfere fon/lajan	**27** transfer funds
retire kat la	**28** remove your card
pran resi a	**29** take your receipt

* nimewo idantifikasyon pèsonèl   * personal identification number

A. Can I pay by ___[1, 2]___ /
   with a ___[3–5]___ ?
B. Yes, you can.

A. What are you doing?
B. { I'm paying the ___[6–15]___ .
    { I'm ___[16–18]___ ing.

A. What are you doing?
B. I'm looking for the ___[19–21]___ .

A. What should I do?
B. ___[22–29]___ .

What household bills do you receive? How much do you pay for the different bills?

Who takes care of the finances in your household? What does that person do?

Do you use ATM machines? If you do, how do you use them?

lèt	**1**	letter
kat postal	**2**	postcard
lèt avyon	**3**	air letter
pake/koli	**4**	package
prenmyè klas	**5**	first class
lèt priyorite	**6**	priority mail
lèt esprès	**7**	express mail
koli postal	**8**	parcel post
lèt sètifye	**9**	certified mail
tenm	**10**	stamp
fèy tenm	**11**	sheet of stamps
woulo tenm	**12**	roll of stamps
kannè tenm	**13**	book of stamps
monnyòdè	**14**	money order
fòm pou chanje adrès	**15**	change-of-address form
fòm pou anwole nan lame	**16**	selective service registration form

fòm aplikasyon pou paspò	**17**	passport application form
anvlòp	**18**	envelope
adrès retounen	**19**	return address
adrès	**20**	mailing address
kòd postal	**21**	zip code
kantite tenm	**22**	stamp
fant pou lèt	**23**	mail slot
anplwaye lapòs	**24**	postal worker/ postal clerk
balans	**25**	scale
machin tenm	**26**	stamp machine
faktè	**27**	letter carrier/ mail carrier
kamyon lapòs	**28**	mail truck
bwat lèt	**29**	mailbox

[1–4]
A. Where are you going?
B. To the post office. I have to mail a/an _____.

[5–9]
A. How do you want to send it?
B. _____, please.

[10–17]
A. Next!
B. I'd like a _____, please.
A. Here you are.

[19–22]
A. Do you want me to mail this letter?
B. Yes, thanks.
A. Oops! You forgot the _____!

How often do you go to the post office? What do you do there?   Tell about the postal system in your country.

THE LIBRARY

BIBLIYOTÈK LA

BOOK 1 of 10 Entries
TITLE: Cat's pajamas
AUTHOR: Bradbury, Ray
CALL NUMBER: 841.238
STATUS: Checked out

Public Library
Amy L. Jackson

katalòg liv nan konpitè	**1** online catalog	(konpitè) lojisyèl	**16** (computer) software
katalòg liv sou kat	**2** card catalog	DVD	**17** DVDs
kat bibliyotèk	**3** library card	seksyon lang etranje	**18** foreign language section
machin fotokopi	**4** copier	liv lang etranje	**19** foreign language books
etajè	**5** shelves	seksyon liv pou referans	**20** reference section
seksyon pou timoun	**6** children's section	lekti sou mikwofilm	**21** microfilm reader
liv pou timoun	**7** children's books	diksyonnè	**22** dictionary
seksyon jounal ak magazin	**8** periodical section	ansiklopedi	**23** encyclopedia
magazin	**9** magazines	atlas	**24** atlas
jounal	**10** newspapers	biwo referans	**25** reference desk
seksyon odyovizyèl	**11** media section	bibliyotekè (referans)	**26** (reference) librarian
liv sou tep	**12** books on tape	kontwa sikilasyon liv	**27** checkout desk
odyo tep yo/kasèt yo	**13** audiotapes	asistan bibliyotekè	**28** library clerk
CD	**14** CDs		
videyotep	**15** videotapes		

[1, 2, 4–28]
A. Excuse me. Where's/Where are the _____?
B. Over there.

[22–24]
A. Excuse me. Where can I find a/an _____?
B. Look in the reference section.
A. Thank you.

[6–12, 17–20]
A. Can you help me? I'm looking for [7, 9, 10, 12, 17, 19] .
B. Look in the [6, 8, 11, 18, 20] over there.
A. Thanks.

Do you go to a library? Where? What does this library have?   Tell about how you use the library.

COMMUNITY INSTITUTIONS

ENSTITISYON KOMINOTE

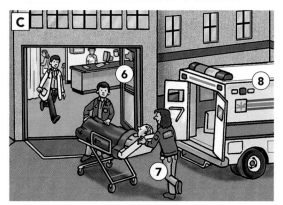

estasyon lapolis	**A** police station	ponpye	**5** firefighter
estasyon ponpye	**B** fire station	sal dijans	**6** emergency room
lopital	**C** hospital	EMT/teknisyen ijans medikal	**7** EMT/paramedic
meri	**D** town hall/city hall	anbilans	**8** ambulance
sant distraksyon	**E** recreation center	majistra	**9** mayor/city manager
baskil	**F** dump	chanm reyinyon	**10** meeting room
gadri	**G** child-care center	jim	**11** gym
sant pou granmoun	**H** senior center	direktè aktivite	**12** activities director
legliz	**I** church	chanm jwèt	**13** game room
sinagòg	**J** synagogue	pisin	**14** swimming pool
moske	**K** mosque	travayè vwari	**15** sanitation worker
tanp	**L** temple	sant resiklaj	**16** recycling center
		anplwaye gadri	**17** child-care worker
èd nan ijans	**1** emergency operator	gadri	**18** nursery
		chanm pou jwe	**19** playroom
ajan lapolis	**2** police officer	anplwaye nan sant granmoun	**20** eldercare worker/ senior care worker
machin polis	**3** police car		
machin ponpye	**4** fire engine		

[A–L]

A. Where are you going?

B. I'm going to the _____.

[1, 2, 5, 7, 12, 15, 17, 20]

A. What do you do?

B. I'm a/an _____.

[3, 4, 8]

A. Do you hear a siren?

B. Yes. There's a/an _____ coming up behind us.

What community institutions are in your city or town? Where are they located?

Which community institutions do you use? When?

KÒ MOUN I

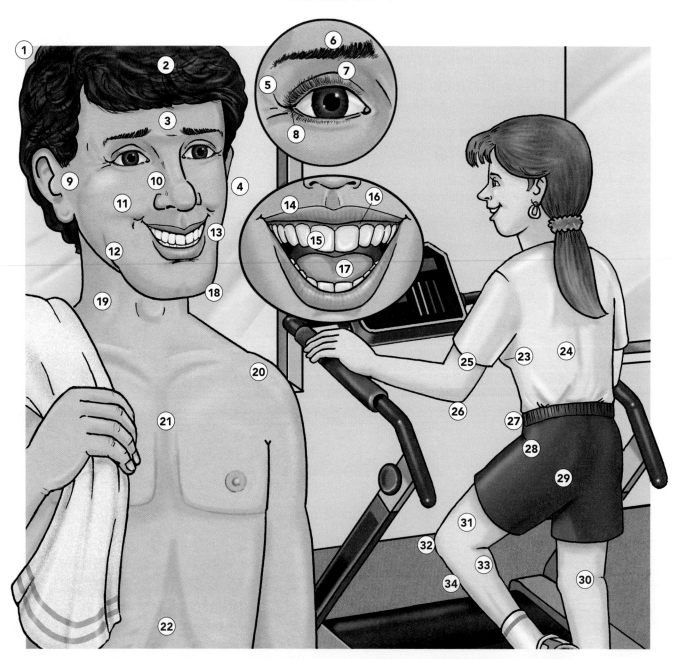

tèt	**1** head	bouch	**13** mouth	bra	**25** arm
cheve	**2** hair	po bouch	**14** lip	koud	**26** elbow
fwon	**3** forehead	dan–dan	**15** tooth–teeth	tay	**27** waist
figi	**4** face	jansiv	**16** gums	ranch	**28** hip
je	**5** eye	lang	**17** tongue	deyè	**29** buttocks
sousi	**6** eyebrow	manton	**18** chin	janm	**30** leg
pòpyè	**7** eyelid	kou	**19** neck	kwis	**31** thigh
pwal je	**8** eyelashes	zepòl	**20** shoulder	jennou	**32** knee
zorèy	**9** ear	pwatrin	**21** chest	mòlèt	**33** calf
nen	**10** nose	vant	**22** abdomen	zo janm	**34** shin
ponmèt	**11** cheek	sen/tete	**23** breast		
machwa	**12** jaw	do	**24** back		

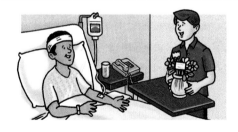

A. My doctor checked my **head** and said everything is okay.
B. I'm glad to hear that.

[1, 3–7, 9–26, 28–34]

A. Ooh!
B. What's the matter?
 { My _____ hurts!
 { My _____ s hurt!

A. Doctor's Office.
B. Hello. This is ..... *(name)* ..... .
 I'm concerned about my _____.
A. Do you want to make an appointment?
B. Yes, please.

Describe yourself as completely as you can.

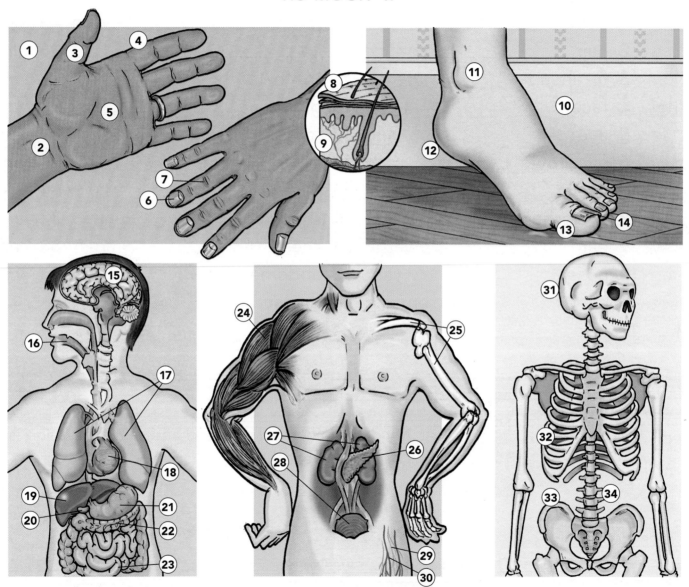

men	**1**	hand	zòtèy	**13**	toe	zo	**25** bones
ponyèt	**2**	wrist	zong pye	**14**	toenail	pankreyas	**26** pancreas
gwo pous	**3**	thumb	sèvo	**15**	brain	ren	**27** kidneys
dwèt	**4**	finger	gòj	**16**	throat	vesi	**28** bladder
pla men	**5**	palm	poumon	**17**	lungs	venn	**29** veins
zong dwèt	**6**	fingernail	kè	**18**	heart	gwo venn	**30** arteries
jwenti dwèt	**7**	knuckle	fwa	**19**	liver	zo tèt	**31** skull
po	**8**	skin	fyèl/sak bil	**20**	gallbladder	kòt	**32** ribcage
nè	**9**	nerve	lestonmak	**21**	stomach	anba vant	**33** pelvis
pye	**10**	foot	gwo trip	**22**	large intestine	jikibb rèldo/	**34** spinal column/
je pye/chevi	**11**	ankle	ti trip	**23**	small intestine	mwèl rèldo	spinal cord
talon	**12**	heel	mis	**24**	muscles		

[1–7, 10–14]
A. What's the matter?
B. I hurt my **hand**.

[1–14]
A. Does your **wrist** hurt when I do THIS?
B. Yes, it does.

[8, 15–34]
A. How am I, Doctor?
B. Well, I'm a little concerned about your **skin**.

Which parts of the body on pages 162–165 are most important at school? at work? when you play your favorite sport?

AILMENTS, SYMPTOMS, AND INJURIES I

MALADI, SENTÒM AK BLESI I

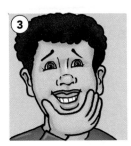
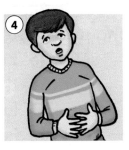
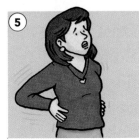

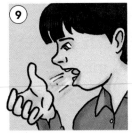

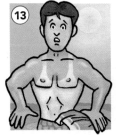

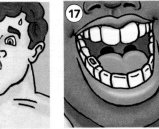
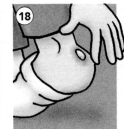
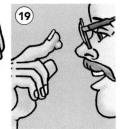

maltèt	**1** headache		kou rèd	**14** stiff neck
malzòrèy	**2** earache		anrimen	**15** runny nose
maldan	**3** toothache		nen senyen	**16** bloody nose
doulè lestomak	**4** stomachache		twou dan	**17** cavity
doulè do	**5** backache		zanpoud	**18** blister
malgòj	**6** sore throat		siy	**19** wart
lafyèv/tanperati	**7** fever/temperature		wòkèt	**20** (the) hiccups
grip	**8** cold		frison	**21** (the) chills
touse	**9** cough		kranp	**22** cramps
enfeksyon	**10** infection		dyare	**23** diarrhea
gratèl	**11** rash		doulè pwatrin	**24** chest pain
piki moustik	**12** insect bite		souf kout	**25** shortness of breath
koutsolèy	**13** sunburn		larenjit	**26** laryngitis

A. What's the matter?
B. I have a/an ___[1–19]___ .

A. What's the matter?
B. I have ___[20–26]___ .

A. How do you feel?
B. Not so good.
A. What's the matter?
B. ....
A. I'm sorry to hear that.

A. Are you okay?
B. Not really. I don't feel very well.
A. What's wrong?
B. ....
A. I'm sorry to hear that.

Tell about a time you had one of these problems.

What do you do when you have a cold?
a stomachache? an insect bite? the hiccups?

AILMENTS, SYMPTOMS, AND INJURIES II

MALADI, SENTÒM AK BLESI II

endispoze	**1**	faint	pye tòdye	**13**	twist
vètij	**2**	dizzy	grate	**14**	scratch
bay lanoze/fè dekonpoze	**3**	nauseous	kòche	**15**	scrape
ayik	**4**	bloated	mètri	**16**	bruise
konjesyonnen	**5**	congested	boule	**17**	burn
bouke	**6**	exhausted	fè mal–fè mal	**18**	hurt–hurt
touse	**7**	cough	koupe–koupe	**19**	cut–cut
etènen	**8**	sneeze	ponyèt foule	**20**	sprain
esoufle	**9**	wheeze	disloke	**21**	dislocate
wote	**10**	burp	kase–kase	**22**	break–broke
vomi	**11**	vomit/throw up	anfle	**23**	swollen
senyen	**12**	bleed	grate	**24**	itchy

A. What's the problem?

B. { I feel _____ [1–4] .
     I'm _____ [5, 6] .

A. Can you describe your symptoms?

B. I'm _____ [7–12] ing a lot.

A. What happened?

B. { I _____ [13–19] ed my ....
     I think I _____ [20–22] ed my ....
     My .... is/are _____ [23, 24] .

Tell about the last time you didn't feel well. What was the matter?

Tell about a time you hurt yourself. What happened? How? What did you do about it?

FIRST AID

PREMYE SEKOU

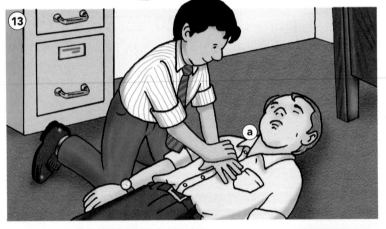

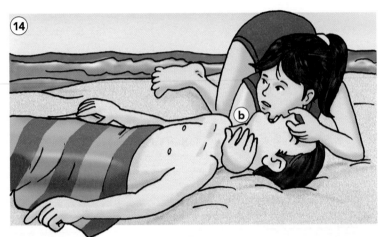

Haitian Creole	#	English
liv premye sekou	1	first-aid manual
bwat premye sekou	2	first-aid kit
bandaj/pansman	3	bandage/Band-Aid™
tanpon/gaz esterilize	4	sterile (dressing) pad
dlo oksijene	5	hydrogen peroxide
pomad antibyotik	6	antibiotic ointment
gaz	7	gauze
adeziv	8	adhesive tape
pens	9	tweezers
bandaj/pansman elastik	10	elastic bandage/Ace™ bandage
aspirin	11	aspirin
analjezik	12	non-aspirin pain reliever

Haitian Creole	#	English
reyannimasyon kadyo pilmonè	13	CPR*
pa gen pou	a	has no pulse
respirasyon bouch nan bouch	14	rescue breathing
li pap respire	b	isn't breathing
manèv Heymlich	15	the Heimlich maneuver
ap toufe	c	is choking
èsplint/2 bwa pou kontwole fakti	16	splint
kase yon dwèt	d	broke a finger
tournikèt	17	tourniquet
I ap senyen	e	is bleeding

* reyaminasyon kadyo-respiratwa * cardiopulmonary resuscitation

A. Do we have any ___[3, 4, 10]___ s/ ___[5–9, 11, 12]___ ?
B. Yes. Look in the first-aid kit.

A. Help! My friend ___[a-e]___ !
B. I can help!
 { I know how to do ___[13-15]___ .
 { I can make a ___[16, 17]___ .

Do you have a first-aid kit? If you do, what's in it? If you don't, where can you buy one?

Tell about a time when you gave or received first aid.

Where can a person learn first aid in your community?

MEDICAL EMERGENCIES AND ILLNESSES

IJANS MEDIKAL AK MALADI

doulè	**1** hurt/injured		gòj enfekte	**14** strep throat
sezisman	**2** in shock		saranpyon	**15** measles
endispoze	**3** unconscious		malmouton	**16** mumps
kout chalè	**4** heatstroke		lawoujòl	**17** chicken pox
brili solèy	**5** frostbite		asm	**18** asthma
kriz kè	**6** heart attack		kansè	**19** cancer
reaksyon alèji	**7** allergic reaction		tristès/depresyon	**20** depression
vale pwazon	**8** swallow poison		dyabèt	**21** diabetes
pran yon dòz depase/	**9** overdose		maladi kè	**22** heart disease
ovèdoz/medikaman	on drugs		tansyon	**23** high blood pressure/
tonbe/te tonbe	**10** fall–fell			hypertension
pran/te pran yon	**11** get–got an electric		tebe/tibèkilez	**24** TB/tuberculosis
chòk elektrik	shock		SIDA*	**25** AIDS*
gripe/flou	**12** the flu/influenza			
enfeksyon nan zòrèy	**13** an ear infection			

* Sendwòm Iminize
Defisitèman Aki

* Acquired Immune
Deficiency Syndrome

A. What's the matter?
B. My .... { is ___[1–3]___ .
has ___[4, 5]___ .
is having a/an ___[6, 7]___ .
A. What's your address?
B. ___(address)___ .

A. What happened?
B. My .... ___[8–11]___ ed.
A. What's your location?
B. ___(address)___ in ___(city/town)___ .

A. My .... is sick.
B. What's the matter?
A. He/She has ___[12–25]___ .
B. I'm sorry to hear that.

Tell about a medical emergency that happened to you or someone you know.

Which illnesses in this lesson are you familiar with?

EGZAMEN MEDIKAL

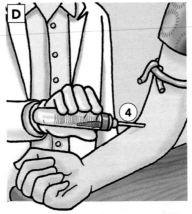

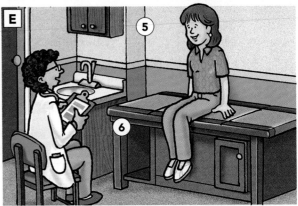

Haitian Creole		English
mezire wotè ak pwa	**A**	measure *your* height and weight
pran tanperati	**B**	take *your* temperature
tcheke tansyon ou	**C**	check *your* blood pressure
pran san	**D**	draw some blood
mande w kesyon sou sante ou	**E**	ask *you* some questions about *your* health
ekzamine je, zorèy, nen, ak gòj ou	**F**	examine *your* eyes, ears, nose, and throat
koute batman kè ou	**G**	listen to *your* heart
pran Eks-re(X-ray)/ radyografi pwatrin	**H**	take a chest X-ray

Haitian Creole		English
balans	**1**	scale
tèmomèt	**2**	thermometer
mezi tansyon	**3**	blood pressure gauge
egiy	**4**	needle
chanm konsiltasyon	**5**	examination room
tab konsiltasyon	**6**	examination table
kat pou li	**7**	eye chart
estetoskop	**8**	stethoscope
machin X-ray/ machin radyografi	**9**	X-ray machine

[A–H]

A. Now I'm going to **measure your height and weight**.
B. All right.

[A–H]

A. What did the doctor/nurse do during the examination?
B. She/He **measured my height and weight**.

[1–3, 5–9]

A. So, how do you like our new **scale**?
B. It's very nice, doctor.

How often do you have a medical exam?

What does the doctor/nurse do?

SWEN MEDIKAL AK SWEN DAN

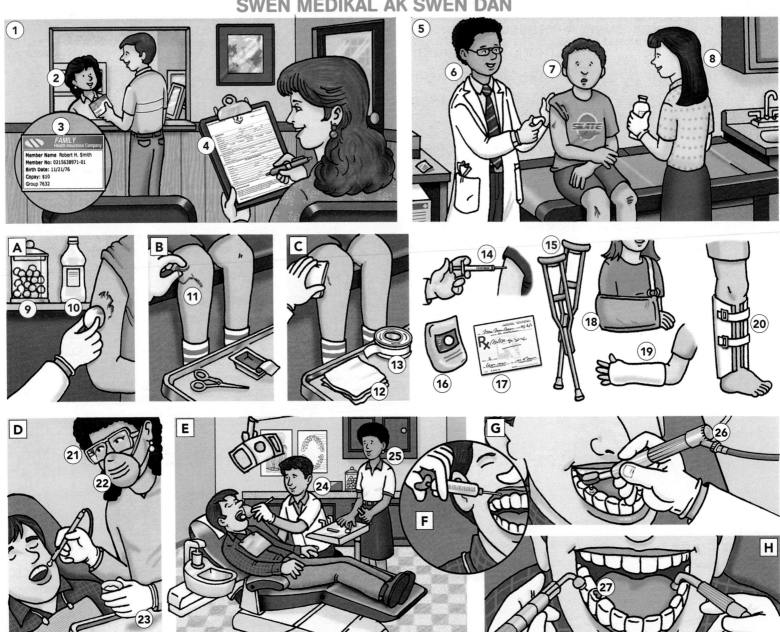

netwaye blese a	**A** clean the wound
fèmen blese a	**B** close the wound
panse blese a	**C** dress the wound
netwaye dan	**D** clean *your* teeth
ekzamine dan ou	**E** examine *your* teeth
bay yon piki anestezi	**F** give *you* a shot of anesthetic/Novocaine™
fouye twou dan an	**G** drill the cavity
ranpli twou dan an	**H** fill the tooth

chanm pou tann	**1** waiting room
resepsyonis	**2** receptionist
kat asirans médico	**3** insurance card

fòm istwa medikal	**4** medical history form
chanm pou konsilte	**5** examination room
doktè	**6** doctor/physician
malad	**7** patient
enfimyè	**8** nurse
boul koton	**9** cotton balls
alkòl	**10** alcohol
kouti/koud yon blese	**11** stitches
gaz	**12** gauze
adeziv	**13** tape
piki	**14** injection/shot
beki	**15** crutches

pake glas	**16** ice pack
preskripsyon	**17** prescription
echap	**18** sling
plat	**19** cast
aparèy	**20** brace
moun ki okipe ijèn	**21** hygienist
mask	**22** mask
gan	**23** gloves
dantis	**24** dentist
èd dantis	**25** dental assistant
frèz	**26** drill
plonbe/dan	**27** filling

A. Now I'm going to ____[A–H]____ .
B. Will it hurt?
A. Just a little.

A. I'm going to { give you (a/an) ____[14–17]____ .
put your ....in a ____[18–20]____ .
B. Okay.

A. I need { ____[9, 10, 12, 13, 23]____ .
a ____[22, 26]____ .
B. Here you are.

Tell about a personal experience you had with a medical or dental procedure.

KONSÈY MEDIKAL

ANNA LOPEZ

EAR NOSE
& THROAT

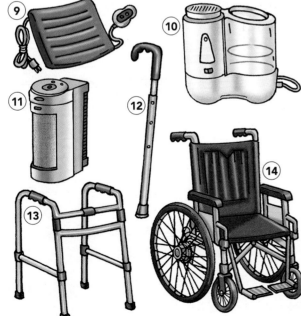

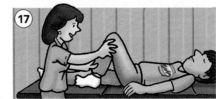

rete kouche	**1**	rest in bed	baton	**12**	cane
bwè likid	**2**	drink fluids	aparèy pou mache	**13**	walker
gagari	**3**	gargle	chèz woulant	**14**	wheelchair
fè dyèt	**4**	go on a diet	egzamen san	**15**	blood work / blood tests
ekzèsis	**5**	exercise			
pran vitamin	**6**	take vitamins	egzamen	**16**	tests
wè yon espesyalis	**7**	see a specialist	terapi pou kò	**17**	physical therapy
trètman ak egiy akiponkti	**8**	get acupuncture	operasyon	**18**	surgery
tanpon k ap bay chalè	**9**	heating pad	bay konsèy	**19**	counseling
aparèy imidite	**10**	humidifier	aparèy pou fikse dan	**20**	braces
aparèy pou netwaye lè a	**11**	air purifier			

A. I think you should ___[1–8]___.
B. I understand.

A. I think { you should use a/an ___[9–14]___.
           { you need ___[15–20]___.
B. I see.

A. What did the doctor say?
B. The doctor thinks { I should ___[1–8]___.
                     { I should use a/an ___[9–14]___.
                     { I need ___[15–20]___.

Tell about medical advice a doctor gave you. What did the doctor say? Did you follow the advice?

MEDICINE

MEDIKAMAN

aspirin	**1** aspirin	gout pou je	**10**	eye drops
grenn pou grip	**2** cold tablets	ponmad	**11**	ointment
vitamin	**3** vitamins	krèm	**12**	cream / creme
siwo tous	**4** cough syrup	losyon	**13**	lotion
analjezik	**5** non-aspirin pain reliever	pilil/grenn	**14**	pill
gout pou tous	**6** cough drops	pastiy	**15**	tablet
pastiy malgòj	**7** throat lozenges	kapsil	**16**	capsule
pastiy kont asid	**8** antacid tablets	tablet	**17**	caplet
vaporizatè nen	**9** decongestant spray / nasal spray	kiyè kafe	**18**	teaspoon
		kiyè tab	**19**	tablespoon

A. What did the doctor say?
B. She told me to take
____[1–4]____ /a ___[5]___ .

A. What did the doctor recommend?
B. He told me to use
____[6–13]____ .

[14–19]

A. What's the dosage?
B. One _____ every four hours.

What medicines in this lesson do you have at home? What other medicines do you have?

What do you take or use for a fever? a headache? a stomachache? a sore throat? a cold? a cough?

Tell about any medicines in your country that are different from the ones in this lesson.

THE HOSPITAL

LOPITAL LA

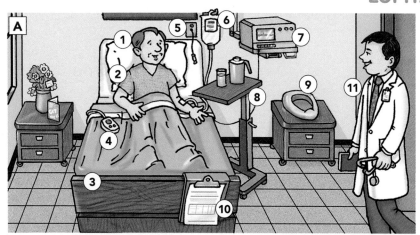

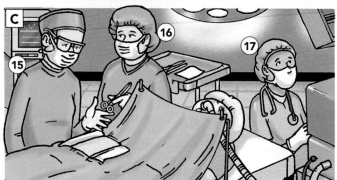

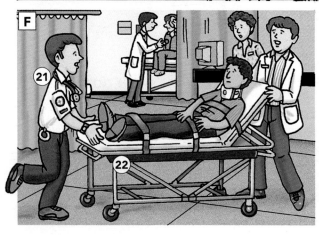

chanm pasyan	**A**	**patient's room**	**estasyon enfimyè**	**B**	**nurse's station**	**chanm ijan**	**F**	**emergency room/ER**
pasyan	1	patient	enfimyè	12	nurse	teknisyen ijans medikal/EMT	21	emergency medical technician/EMT
chemiz lopital	2	hospital gown	kontwolè rejim moun	13	dietitian			
kabann lopital	3	hospital bed	anplwaye lopital	14	orderly	kabann woulant	22	gurney
kontwòl kabann	4	bed control						
sonnèt	5	call button	**sal operasyon**	**C**	**operating room**	**depatman radyoloji**	**G**	**radiology department**
boutèy sewòm	6	I.V.				teknisyen radyografi	23	X-ray technician
aparèy kontwòl siy lavi	7	vital signs monitor	chirijyen	15	surgeon			
			enfimyè chirijyen	16	surgical nurse	radyològ	24	radiologist
tab kabann	8	bed table	anestezyolojis	17	anesthesiologist			
basen	9	bed pan	**chanm pou tann**	**D**	**waiting room**	**laboratwa**	**H**	**laboratory/lab**
fèy sante/ dosye medikal	10	medical chart	volontè	18	volunteer	teknisyen laboratwa	25	lab technician
doktè	11	doctor/ physician	**sal akouchman**	**E**	**birthing room/ delivery room**			
			obstetrisyen	19	obstetrician			
			fanm saj	20	midwife/ nurse-midwife			

A. This is your _____[2–10]_____.
B. I see.

A. Do you work here?
B. Yes. I'm a/an _____[11–21, 23–25]_____.

A. Where's the _____[11–21, 23–25]_____?
B. She's/He's { in the _____[A, C–H]_____.
              at the _____[B]_____.

Tell about an experience you or a family member had in the hospital.

IJYÈN PÈSONÈL

bwose dan m   **A**   **brush** *my* **teeth**

bwòsdan   **1**   toothbrush

pat   **2**   toothpaste

pase fil nan dan   **B**   **floss** *my* **teeth**

fil dantè   **3**   dental floss

gagari	**C**	**gargle**	
lavay bouch	**4**	mouthwash	
benyen	**D**	**bathe/take a bath**	
savon	**5**	soap	
kim pou benyen	**6**	bubble bath	
pran yon douch	**E**	**take a shower**	
chapo beny	**7**	shower cap	
lave cheve _m_	**F**	**wash _my_ hair**	
chanpou	**8**	shampoo	
kondisyonè	**9**	conditioner	
seche cheve _m_	**G**	**dry _my_ hair**	
aparèy pou seche cheve	**10**	hair dryer/blow dryer	
penyen tèt _mwen_	**H**	**comb _my_ hair**	
peny	**11**	comb	
bwose tèt _mwen_	**I**	**brush _my_ hair**	
bwòs tèt	**12**	brush	
fè bab	**J**	**shave**	
krèm pou bab	**13**	shaving cream	
razwa	**14**	razor	
razwa elektrik	**15**	electric shaver	

fè zong _mwen_	**K**	**do _my_ nails**	
lim zong an fè	**16**	nail file	
tay zong	**17**	nail clipper	
sizo	**18**	scissors	
vèni pou zong	**19**	nail polish	
mete . . .	**L**	**put on . . .**	
dezodoran	**20**	deodorant	
pafen/kolòy	**21**	cologne/perfume	
poud	**22**	powder	
krèm solèy	**23**	sunscreen	
makiye	**M**	**put on makeup**	
fondten/fa jou	**24**	blush/rouge	
makiyaj pou arebò zye	**25**	eyeliner	
makiyaj popyè	**26**	eye shadow	
maskara	**27**	mascara	
woujalèv	**28**	lipstick	
netwaye soulye mwen yo	**N**	**polish _my_ shoes**	
blakbòl/ekla	**29**	shoe polish	
lasèt	**30**	shoelaces	

[A–K, L (20–23), M, N]
A. What are you doing?
B. I'm _____ing.

[1, 7, 10–12, 14–18, 30]
A. Excuse me. Where can I find _____(s)?
B. They're in the next aisle.

[2–6, 8, 9, 13, 19–29]
A. Excuse me. Where can I find _____?
B. It's in the next aisle.

Which of these personal care products do you use?

You're going on a trip. Make a list of the personal care products you need to take with you.

SWEN BEBE

bay manje	**A**	**feed**	**benyen**	**C**	**bathe**
manje bebe	1	baby food	chanpou bebe	14	baby shampoo
			aplikatè	15	cotton swab
bavèt	2	bib	losyon bebe	16	baby lotion
bibwon	3	bottle			
tetin	4	nipple	**kenbe**	**D**	**hold**
lèt an poud	5	formula	sison	17	pacifier
vitamin an likid	6	(liquid) vitamins	jansivèt	18	teething ring
chanje kouchèt bebe a	**B**	**change the baby's diaper**	**enfimyè**	**E**	**nurse**
kouchèt papye	7	disposable diaper	**rad**	**F**	**dress**
kouchèt twal	8	cloth diaper	**balanse**	**G**	**rock**
zepeng kouchèt	9	diaper pin	gadri	19	child-care center
papye ijenik pou bebe	10	(baby) wipes	anplwaye gadri	20	child-care worker
poud pou bebe	11	baby powder	chèz dodin	21	rocking chair
pantalon kouchèt pou aprann al nan twalèt	12	training pants	**li**	**H**	**read to**
			kazye	22	cubby
ponmad	13	ointment	**jwe ak**	**I**	**play with**
			jwèt	23	toys

A. What are you doing?
B. { I'm ___[A, C–I]___ ing the baby.
{ I'm ___[B]___ ing.

A. Do we need anything from the store?
B. Yes. We need some more { ___[2–4, 7–9, 15, 17, 18]___ s.
{ ___[1, 5, 6, 10–14, 16]___ .

In your opinion, which are better: cloth diapers or disposable diapers? Why?

Tell about baby products in your country.

SCHOOL SUBJECTS

PWOGRAM LEKÒL

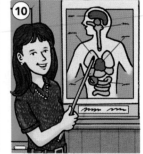

matematik	**1**	math/mathematics	espayòl	**12**	Spanish
angle	**2**	English	franse	**13**	French
istwa	**3**	history	ekonomi domestik	**14**	home economics
jewografi	**4**	geography	atelye atizana	**15**	industrial arts/shop
gouvènman	**5**	government	edikasyon biznis	**16**	business education
syans	**6**	science	edikasyon fizik	**17**	physical education/ P.E.
byoloji	**7**	biology			
chimi	**8**	chemistry	leson kondi	**18**	driver's education/ driver's ed
fizik	**9**	physics			
sante	**10**	health	bèlte	**19**	art
syans konpitè	**11**	computer science	mizik	**20**	music

A. What do you have next period?
B. **Math**. How about you?
A. **English**.
B. There's the bell. I've got to go.

What is/was your favorite subject? Why?

In your opinion, what's the most interesting subject? the most difficult subject? Why do you think so?

AKTIVITE APRE KLAS

òkès lekòl	**1**	band	liv souvni lekòl	**10**	yearbook
òkès klasik	**2**	orchestra	magazin literè	**11**	literary magazine
koral	**3**	choir/chorus	ekip odyo ak videyo	**12**	A.V. crew
teyat	**4**	drama	klib deba	**13**	debate club
foutbòl Ameriken	**5**	football	klib konpitè	**14**	computer club
ekip kap chofe	**6**	cheerleading/ pep squad	klib entènasyonal	**15**	international club
etidyan gouvènman sipòte	**7**	student government	klib echèk	**16**	chess club
sèvis kominote	**8**	community service			
jounal lekòl	**9**	school newspaper			

[1–6]

A. Are you going home right after school?

B. No. I have **band** practice.

[7–16]

A. What are you going to do after school today?

B. I have a **student government** meeting.

What extracurricular activities do/did you participate in?

Which extracurricular activities in this lesson are there in schools in your country? What other activities are there?

MATEMATIK

Arithmetic   Aritmetik

$$2+1=3 \qquad 8-3=5 \qquad 4\times2=8 \qquad 10\div2=5$$

addition	subtraction	multiplication	division
adisyon	soustraksyon	miltiplikasyon	divizyon

2 **plus** 1 **equals*** 3.   8 **minus** 3 **equals*** 5.   4 **times** 2 **equals*** 8.   10 **divided by** 2 **equals*** 5.

* Ou ka di tou: **se**

A. How much is *two plus one*?
B. *Two plus one* equals / is *three*.

Make conversations for the arithmetic problems above and others.

Fractions   Fraksyon

one quarter / one fourth	one third	one half / half	two thirds	three quarters / three fourths

A. Is this on sale?
B. Yes. It's _____ off the regular price.

A. Is the gas tank almost empty?
B. It's about _____ full.

Percents *Pousantaj*

10%
ten
percent

50%
fifty
percent

75%
seventy-five
percent

100%
one-hundred
percent

A. How did you do on the test?
B. I got _____ percent of the answers right.

A. What's the weather forecast?
B. There's a _____ percent chance of rain.

Types of Math *Kalite matematik*

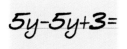

$5y - 5y + 3 =$

algebra
aljèb

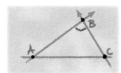

geometry
jewometri

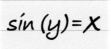

$\sin(y) = x$

trigonometry
trigonometri

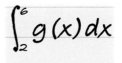

$\int_{2}^{6} g(x)\,dx$

calculus
kalkil

statistics
estatistik

A. What math course are you taking this year?
B. I'm taking _____.

Are you good at math?

What math courses do/did you take in school?

Tell about something you bought on sale. How much off the regular price was it?

Research and discuss: What percentage of people in your country live in cities? live on farms? work in factories?

MEZI AK FÒM JEWOMETRI

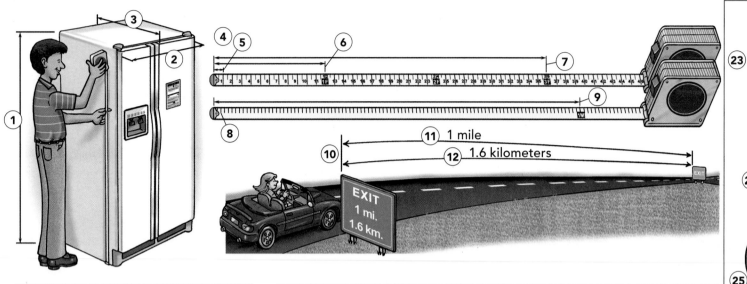

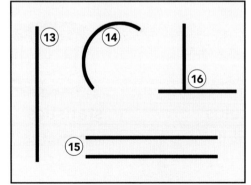

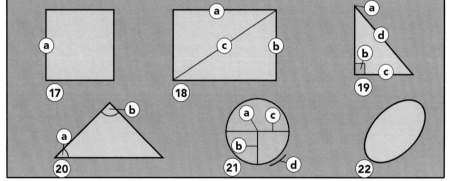

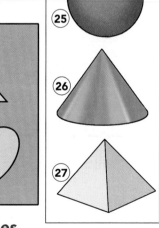

Mezi		Measurements	mèt	**7**	yard	Liy		Lines
wotè	**1**	height	santimèt	**8**	centimeter	liy dwat	**13**	straight line
lajè	**2**	width	mèt	**9**	meter	liy koub	**14**	curved line
pwofondè	**3**	depth	distans	**10**	distance	liy paralèl	**15**	parallel lines
longè	**4**	length	mil	**11**	mile	liy pèpandikilè	**16**	perpendicular lines
pous	**5**	inch	kilomèt	**12**	kilometer			
pye–pye	**6**	foot–feet						

Fòm Jewometri	**Geometric Shapes**		sèk	**21** circle
kare	**17** square		sant	**a** center
kote	**a** side		reyon	**b** radius
rektang	**18** rectangle		dyamèt	**c** diameter
longè	**a** length		sikonferans	**d** circumference
lajè	**b** width		elips/oval	**22** ellipse/oval
dyagonal	**c** diagonal		**Fòm Solid**	**Solid Figures**
triyang rektang	**19** right triangle		kib	**23** cube
somè	**a** apex		silend	**24** cylinder
ang dwa	**b** right angle		esfè	**25** sphere
baz	**c** base		kòn	**26** cone
ipoteniz	**d** hypotenuse		piramid	**27** pyramid
triyang izosèl	**20** isosceles triangle			
ang egi	**a** acute angle			
ang obti	**b** obtuse angle			

[1–9]
A. What's the ___[1–4]___?
B. .... ___[5–9]___(s).

[11–12]
A. What's the distance?
B. .... _____(s).

> 1 inch (1") = 2.54 centimeters (cm)
> 1 foot (1') = 0.305 meters (m)
> 1 yard (1 yd.) = 0.914 meters (m)
> 1 mile (mi.) = 1.6 kilometers (km)

[17–22]
A. What shape is this?
B. It's a/an _____.

[23–27]
A. What figure is this?
B. It's a/an _____.

[13–27]
A. This painting is magnificent!
B. Hmm. I don't think so. It just looks like a lot of _____s and _____s to me!

LANG ANGLE AK KONPOZISYON

Types of Sentences & Parts of Speech　　**Kalite Fraz Ak Pati Diskou**

A Students study in the new library.
1 2 3 4 5

C Read page nine.

B Do they study hard?
6 7

D This cake is fantastic!

fraz deklare	**A** declarative	non	**1** noun	adjektif	**5** adjective
fraz entewogativ	**B** interrogative	vèb	**2** verb	pwonon	**6** pronoun
fraz kòmande	**C** imperative	prepozisyon	**3** preposition	advèb	**7** adverb
fraz eksklamantwa	**D** exclamatory	atik	**4** article		

A. What type of sentence is this?
B. It's a/an __[A–D]__ sentence.

A. What part of speech is this?
B. It's a/an __[1–7]__ .

Punctuation Marks & the Writing Process

Siy Pontiyasyon Ak Pwosesis Redaksyon

pwen	**8** period	depwen	**14** colon
pwen	**9** question	pwen vigil	**15** semi-colon
dentèwogasyon	mark	brase lide	**16** brainstorm
pwen	**10** exclamation		ideas
desklamasyon	point	òganize lide	**17** organize *my*
vigil	**11** comma		ideas
apostwòf	**12** apostrophe	ekri yon	**18** write a first
gimè	**13** quotation marks	premye kopi	draft

tit	**a** title
paragraf	**b** paragraph
fè koreksyon	**19** make corrections/
	revise/edit
bay fidbak	**20** get feedback
ekri yon	**21** write a final
dènnye kopi	copy/rewrite

A. Did you find any mistakes?
B. Yes. You forgot to put a/an ___[8–15]___ in this sentence.

A. Are you working on your composition?
B. Yes. I'm ___[16–21]___ing.

LITERATI AK EKRITI

fiksyon/ istwa imajine	**1** fiction		atik jounal	**11** newspaper article
woman	**2** novel		editoryal	**12** editorial
ti istwa	**3** short story		lèt	**13** letter
powèm	**4** poetry/poems		kat postal	**14** postcard
istwa vre	**5** non-fiction		nòt	**15** note
byografi	**6** biography		envitasyon	**16** invitation
otobyografi	**7** autobiography		lèt remèsiman	**17** thank-you note
redaksyon	**8** essay		memo	**18** memo
rapò	**9** report		imèl	**19** e-mail
atik magazin	**10** magazine article		mesaj enstantane	**20** instant message

A. What are you doing?

B. I'm writing {
 [1, 4, 5].
 a/an [2, 3, 6–20].
}

What kind of literature do you like to read? What are some of your favorite books? Who is your favorite author?

Do you like to read newspapers and magazines? Which ones do you read?

Do you sometimes send or receive letters, postcards, notes, e-mail, or instant messages? Tell about the people you communicate with, and how.

JEWOGRAFI

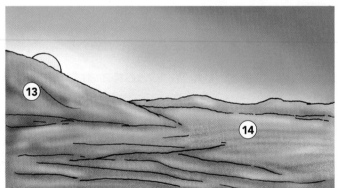

forè/bwa	**1**	forest/woods	mòn sab	**13**	dune/sand dune
ti mòn	**2**	hill	dezè	**14**	desert
yon gwoup mòn	**3**	mountain range	rakbwa	**15**	jungle
pwen tèt mòn	**4**	mountain peak	bò lanmè	**16**	seashore/shore
vale	**5**	valley	bè	**17**	bay
lak	**6**	lake	lanmè	**18**	ocean
plèn yo	**7**	plains	zile	**19**	island
savann	**8**	meadow	prèskil	**20**	peninsula
ti kouran dlo	**9**	stream/brook	fore	**21**	rainforest
letan	**10**	pond	rivyè	**22**	river
plato	**11**	plateau	chit dlo/kaskad	**23**	waterfall
kannyon	**12**	canyon			

A. ⎰ This is a beautiful _____!
⎱ These are beautiful _____s!

B. I agree. It's/They're magnificent!

Tell about the geography of your country. Describe the different geographic features.

Have you seen some of the geographic features in this lesson? Which ones? Where?

SYANS

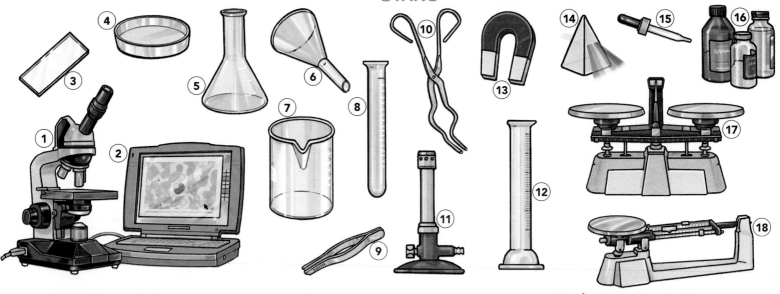

Ekipman Syantifik	Science Equipment
mikwoskòp	**1** microscope
konpitè	**2** computer
mòso glas mete nan mikwoskòp	**3** slide
ti asyèt plastik nan labowatwa	**4** Petri dish
flas	**5** flask
antonwa	**6** funnel
gòde	**7** beaker
tib pou fè tès/egzamen	**8** test tube
pens	**9** forceps
ti pens	**10** crucible tongs
fou a gaz	**11** Bunsen burner
silend ki gen mezi	**12** graduated cylinder
leman	**13** magnet

pris	**14** prism
konngout	**15** dropper
pwodui chimik	**16** chemicals
balans	**17** balance
balans	**18** scale

Methòd Syantifik La — The Scientific Method

di pwoblèm la	**A** state the problem
fòme yon ipotèz	**B** form a hypothesis
planifye yon pwosedi	**C** plan a procedure
fè yon pwosedi	**D** do a procedure
fè obzèvasyon	**E** make/record observations
fè konklizyon	**F** draw conclusions

A. What do we need to do this procedure?
B. We need a/an/the ___[1–18]___ .

A. How is your experiment coming along?
B. I'm getting ready to ___[A–F]___ .

Do you have experience with the scientific equipment in this lesson? Tell about it.

What science courses do/did you take in school?

Think of an idea for a science experiment.
What question about science do you want to answer? State the problem.
What do you think will happen in the experiment? Form a hypothesis.
How can you test your hypothesis? Plan a procedure.

OCCUPATIONS I

OKIPASYON I

kontab	**1** accountant		komèsant	**11** businesswoman
aktè	**2** actor		machann vyann	**12** butcher
aktris	**3** actress		chapantye	**13** carpenter
atis pent	**4** artist		kesye	**14** cashier
ajistè	**5** assembler		kwizinye	**15** chef/cook
moun ki gade timoun	**6** babysitter		anplwaye gadri	**16** child day-care worker
boulanje	**7** baker		enjènyè konpitè	**17** computer software engineer
kwafè	**8** barber		ouvriye nan konstriksyon	**18** construction worker
mason	**9** bricklayer/ mason			
biznismann/komèsan	**10** businessman			

[1–5]

A. What do you do?

B. I'm an **accountant**.

[6–18]

A. What do you do?

B. I'm a **babysitter**.

Which of these occupations do you think is the most interesting? Why?

OKIPASYON II

jeran	**1**	custodian / janitor
sekretè k ap rantre enfòmasyon	**2**	data entry clerk
gason livrezon	**3**	delivery person
travayè waf	**4**	dockworker
travayè faktori	**5**	factory worker
fèmye	**6**	farmer
ponpye	**7**	firefighter
pechè	**8**	fisher
anplwaye nan sèvis manje	**9**	food-service worker
kontremèt	**10**	foreman
jadinye	**11**	gardener / landscaper
koutirye / koutiryèz	**12**	garment worker
kwafèz	**13**	hairdresser
èd / asistan enfimyè	**14**	health-care aide / attendant
èd enfimyè nan kay	**15**	home health aide / home attendant
metrès kay	**16**	homemaker

A. What do you do?
B. I'm a **custodian**.

Which of these occupations do you think is the most difficult? Why?

OCCUPATIONS III

OKIPASYON III

mennajè	**1** housekeeper		mesaje	**9** messenger/ courier
avoka	**2** lawyer		moun k ap ede demenaje	**10** mover
operatè aparèy	**3** machine operator		bòs pent	**11** painter
faktè	**4** mail carrier/ letter carrier		famasyen	**12** pharmacist
manadjè	**5** manager		fotograf	**13** photographer
estetisyèn maniki	**6** manicurist		pilot avyon	**14** pilot
mekanisyen	**7** mechanic		jandam/ajan lapolis	**15** police officer
asistan medikal	**8** medical assistant/ physician assistant		resepsyonis	**16** receptionist

A. What's your occupation?
B. I'm a **housekeeper**.
A. A **housekeeper**?
B. Yes. That's right.

Which of these occupations do you think is the most important?   Why?

reparatè **1** repairperson

vandèz/komi magazen **2** salesperson

travayè vwari **3** sanitation worker/ trash collector

sekretè **4** secretary

gadyen sekirite **5** security guard

brikolè gason **6** serviceman

brikolè fanm **7** servicewoman

anplwaye depo **8** stock clerk

mèt magazen **9** store owner/ shopkeeper

sipèvizè **10** supervisor

tayè **11** tailor

pwofesè/mèt **12** teacher/ instructor

tradiktè/ entèprèt **13** translator/ interpreter

chofè kamyon **14** truck driver

veterinè **15** veterinarian/vet

gason **16** waiter/server

madmwazèl **17** waitress/server

soudè/wèldè **18** welder

A. What do you do?
B. I'm a **repairperson**. How about you?
A. I'm a **secretary**.

Do you work? What's your occupation? What are the occupations of the people in your family?

JOB SKILLS AND ACTIVITIES I

KONESANS TRAVAY AK AKTIVITE I

fè teyat	**1**	act	klase	**10**	file
ajiste pyès/	**2**	assemble	pilote *yon avyon*	**11**	fly *an airplane*
sanble pyès		*components*	plante *legim*	**12**	grow *vegetables*
ede *malad*	**3**	assist *patients*	siveye *batisman*	**13**	guard *buildings*
monte/konstwi	**4**	build *things*/			
bagay		construct *things*	dirije *yon restoran*	**14**	manage *a restaurant*
netwaye	**5**	clean	koupe *gazon*	**15**	mow *lawns*
kwit	**6**	cook	travay sou *machin*	**16**	operate *equipment*
livre *pitza*	**7**	deliver *pizzas*			
desinen	**8**	draw			
kondi yon *kamyon*	**9**	drive *a truck*			

A. Can you **act**?
B. Yes, I can.

Can you do any of these activities? Which ones?

JOB SKILLS AND ACTIVITIES II

KONESANS TRAVAY AK AKTIVITE II

pentire	**1**	paint
prepare *manje*	**2**	prepare *food*
repare/fiske *bagay*	**3**	repair *things*/ fix *things*
vann *machin*	**4**	sell *cars*
sèvi *manje*	**5**	serve *food*
koud	**6**	sew
pale *Panyòl*	**7**	speak *Spanish*
sipèvizè *moun*	**8**	supervise *people*
okipe *granmoun*	**9**	take care of *elderly people*

konte tout pwovizyon	**10**	take inventory
anseye	**11**	teach
tradui	**12**	translate
tape	**13**	type
sèvi ak yon kèsye	**14**	use *a cash register*
lave *vesèl*	**15**	wash *dishes*
ekri	**16**	write

A. Do you know how to **paint**?
B. Yes, I do.

Tell about your job skills. What can you do?

CHÈCHE TRAVAY

Diferan kalite anons pou travay/djòb	**Types of Job Ads**
siy pou travay	**1** help wanted sign
anons pou djòb/travay	**2** job notice / job announcement
anons ki klase	**3** classified ad / want ad

Anons travay abrejions	**Job Ad Abbreviations**
travay tout tan	**4** full-time
travay enpetan	**5** part-time
lib	**6** available
è	**7** hour
Lendi a Vandredi	**8** Monday through Friday
aswè	**9** evenings
anvan	**10** previous
eksperyans	**11** experience
egzije	**12** required
ekselan	**13** excellent

Sèche travay	**Job Search**
reponn yon anons	**A** respond to an ad
mande enfòmasyon	**B** request information
mande yon antrevi	**C** request an interview
prepare yon dosye/rezime	**D** prepare a resume
abiye byen	**E** dress appropriately
ranpli yon aplikasyon	**F** fill out an application (form)
ale nan yon antrevi	**G** go to an interview
pale osijè sa ou konnen ak kalifikasyon ou	**H** talk about your skills and qualifications
pale osijè eksperyans ou	**I** talk about your experience
mande salè a	**J** ask about the salary
mande kesyon sou benefis yo	**K** ask about the benefits
ekri yon lèt remèsiman	**L** write a thank-you note
gen travay la	**M** get hired

A. How did you find your job?
B. I found it through a ___[1–3]___ .

A. How was your job interview?
B. It went very well.
A. Did you ___[D–F, H–M]___ ?
B. Yes, I did.

Tell about a job you are familiar with. What are the skills and qualifications required for the job? What are the hours? What is the salary?

Tell about how people you know found their jobs.

Tell about your own experience with a job search or a job interview.

THE FACTORY

FABRIK LA

pandil prezans	**1** time clock	machin transpò	**13** forklift
kat lè	**2** time cards	koli lou elevatè machandiz	**14** freight elevator
vestyè	**3** locker room	tablo nòt sendika	**15** union notice
chenn asanblaj	**4** (assembly) line	bwat sijesyon	**16** suggestion box
travayè faktori	**5** (factory) worker	depatman ekspedisyon	**17** shipping department
estasyon travay	**6** work station		
sipèvizè liy	**7** line supervisor	anplwaye ekspedisyon	**18** shipping clerk
sipèvizè kalite travay	**8** quality control supervisor		
		charyo	**19** hand truck/dolly
machin	**9** machine	platfòm chajman	**20** loading dock
tapi woulan	**10** conveyor belt	biwo pewòl	**21** payroll office
depo	**11** warehouse	biwo pèsonnèl	**22** personnel office
anbalè	**12** packer		

A. Excuse me. I'm a new employee.
Where's / Where are the _____?
B. Next to / Near / In / On the _____.

A. Where's *Tony*?
B. *He's* in / on / at / next to / near the _____.

Are there any factories where you live? What kind? What are the working conditions there?

What products do factories in your country produce?

THE CONSTRUCTION SITE

KOTE Y AP BATI

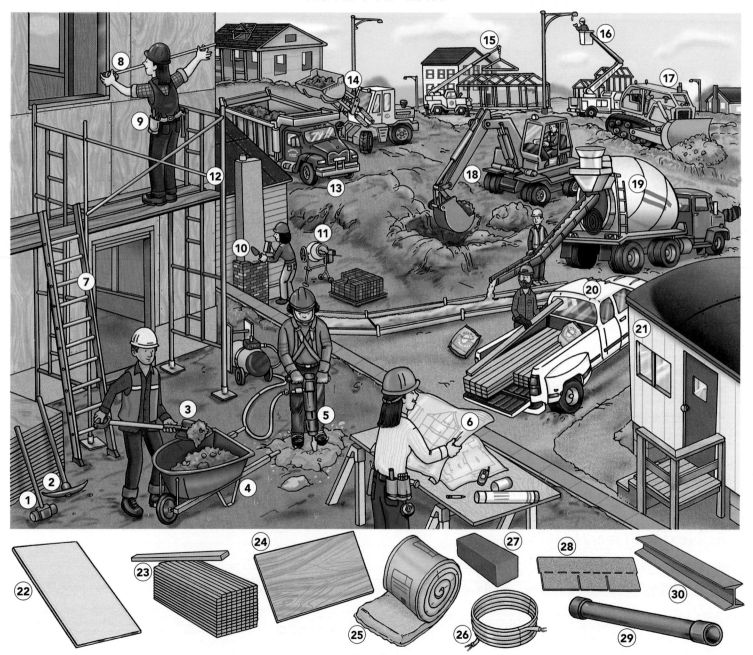

mato mas	**1**	sledgehammer	machin elevatè travayè	**16**	cherry picker
pikwa	**2**	pickax	bouldozè	**17**	bulldozer
pèl	**3**	shovel	pèl mekanik	**18**	backhoe
bourèt	**4**	wheelbarrow	malaksè	**19**	concrete mixer truck
mato konpresè	**5**	jackhammer/ pneumatic drill	pikòp	**20**	pickup truck
plan batisman	**6**	blueprints	trelè	**21**	trailer
nechèl	**7**	ladder	fèy panno	**22**	drywall
riban mezi	**8**	tape measure	bwa/planch	**23**	wood/lumber
senti zouti	**9**	toolbelt	playwoud	**24**	plywood
tiwèl	**10**	trowel	izolan	**25**	insulation
malaksè	**11**	cement mixer	fil elektrik	**26**	wire
echafo	**12**	scaffolding	brik	**27**	brick
kamyon baskil	**13**	dump truck	chingèl	**28**	shingle
lodè	**14**	front-end loader	fè tiyo	**29**	pipe
machin elevatè	**15**	crane	pout metal	**30**	girder/beam

A. Could you get me that/those ___[1–10]___?
B. Sure.

A. Watch out for that ___[11–21]___!
B. Oh! Thanks for the warning!

A. Do we have enough ___[22–26]___ / ___[27–30]___s?
B. I think so.

What building materials is your home made of?

Describe a construction site near your home or school. Tell about the construction equipment and the materials.

JOB SAFETY

PWOTÈJ NAN TRAVAY

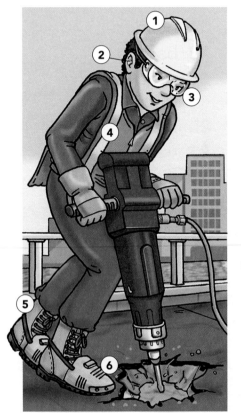

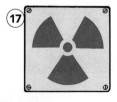

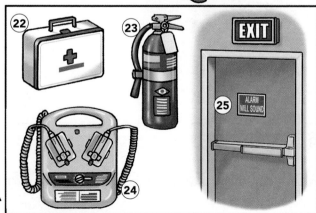

DANGER

CAUTION
HAZARDOUS
AREA

EXIT

ALARM
WILL SOUND

AIR C

27

kas pou pwoteje	**1** hard hat/helmet		ka pran dife	**14** flammable
bouchon zòrèy	**2** earplugs		pwazon	**15** poisonous
linèt pou pwoteje	**3** goggles		kowozif	**16** corrosive
vès pwotèj	**4** safety vest		radyoaktiv	**17** radioactive
bòt pwotèj	**5** safety boots		danje	**18** dangerous
pwoteksyon zòtèy	**6** toe guard		danje	**19** hazardous
sipò do	**7** back support		danje chimik	**20** biohazard
pwotèj zòrèy	**8** safety earmuffs		danje elektrik	**21** electrical hazard
filè	**9** hairnet		bwat prenmye swen	**22** first-aid kit
mask	**10** mask		ekstentè	**23** fire extinguisher
gan latèks	**11** latex gloves		defibrilatè	**24** defibrillator
respiratè	**12** respirator		pòtsekoui/sòti ijans	**25** emergency exit
linèt pou pwoteje	**13** safety glasses			

A. Don't forget to wear your __[1–13]__ !
B. Thanks for reminding me.

A. Be careful!
{
That material is __[14–17]__ !
That machine is __[18]__ !
That work area is __[19]__ !
That's a __[20]__ !/That's an __[21]__ !
}
B. Thanks for the warning.

A. Where's the __[22–25]__ ?
B. It's over there.

Do you/Did you ever use any of the safety equipment in this lesson? When? Where?

Where do you see safety equipment in your community?

PUBLIC TRANSPORTATION

TRANSPÒ PIBLIK

bis	**A**	**bus**	orè	**15**	schedule / timetable
estòp bis	**1**	bus stop	platfòm	**16**	platform
wout bis	**2**	bus route	ray	**17**	track
pasaje	**3**	passenger	chofè tren	**18**	conductor
lajan otobis	**4**	(bus) fare			
transfè	**5**	transfer	**sòbwe**	**C**	**subway**
chofè bis	**6**	bus driver	estasyon sòbwe	**19**	subway station
estasyon bis	**7**	bus station	tokenn sòbwe	**20**	(subway) token
kontwa gichè	**8**	ticket counter	pasaj sou platfòm	**21**	turnstile
tikè	**9**	ticket	kat sòbwe	**22**	fare card
konpatman malèt	**10**	baggage compartment	machin kat sòbwe	**23**	fare card machine
			taksi	**D**	**taxi**
tren	**B**	**train**	estasyon taksi	**24**	taxi stand
estasyon tren	**11**	train station	taksi	**25**	taxi / cab
gichè / fenèt tikè	**12**	ticket window	kontè	**26**	meter
tablo arrive ak sòti	**13**	arrival and departure board	chofè taksi	**27**	cab driver / taxi driver
gichè enfòmasyon	**14**	information booth	**bato navèt**	**E**	**ferry**

[A–E]
A. How are you going to get there?
B. { I'm going to take the ____[A–C, E] .
  { I'm going to take a ____[D] .

[1, 7, 8, 10–19, 21, 23–25]
A. Excuse me. Where's the ____?
B. Over there.

How do you get to different places in your community? Describe public transportation where you live.

In your country, can you travel far by train or by bus? Where can you go? How much do tickets cost? Describe the buses and trains.

PREPOSITIONS OF MOTION

PREPOZISYON MOUVMAN

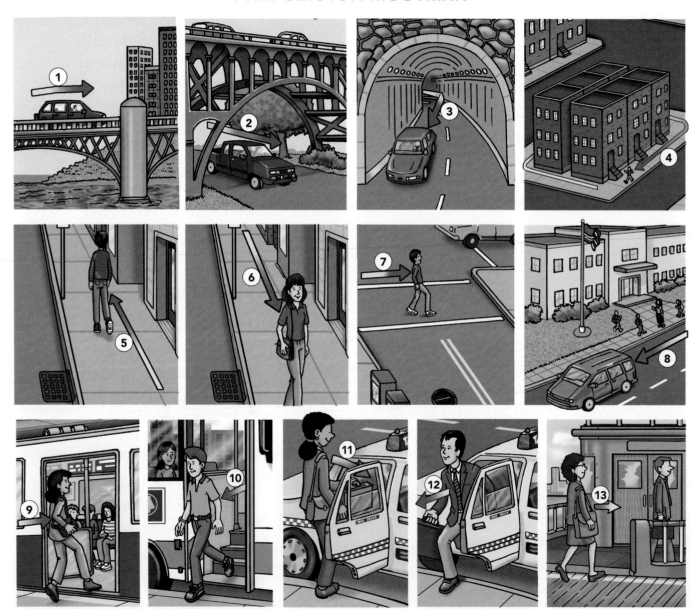

anwo pon an	**1**	over the bridge
anba pon an	**2**	under the bridge
atravè tinèl la	**3**	through the tunnel
toupre kwen an	**4**	around the corner
anwo lari a	**5**	up the street
anba lari a	**6**	down the street
nan tout lari a	**7**	across the street

depase *lekòl* la	**8**	past the *school*
sou	**9**	on
etenn/kanpe lwen	**10**	off
nan	**11**	into
deyò	**12**	out of
nan	**13**	onto

[1–8]
A. Go **over** the bridge.
B. **Over** the bridge?
A. Yes.

[9–13]
A. I can't talk right now. I'm getting **on** a train.
B. You're getting **on** a train?
A. Yes. I'll call you later.

What places do you go past on your way to school?

Tell how to get to different places from your home or your school.

SIY SIKILASYON AK DIREKSYON

Siy Sikilasyon	**Traffic Signs**
rete	**1** stop
pa vire agòch	**2** no left turn
pa vire adwat	**3** no right turn
pa kase tèt tounen	**4** no U-turn
vire dwat sèlman	**5** right turn only
pa rantre	**6** do not enter
sans inik	**7** one way
enpas	**8** dead end/no outlet
pyeton ap travèse	**9** pedestrian crossing
tren kap travèse	**10** railroad crossing
travase lekòl	**11** school crossing
wout la kontre	**12** merging traffic
kite lòt machin pase	**13** yield
detou	**14** detour
li glise lè li mouye	**15** slippery when wet
pakin pou moun andikape sèlman	**16** handicapped parking only

Direksyon bousòl	**Compass Directions**
nò	**17** north
sid	**18** south
wès	**19** west
ès	**20** east

Entriksyon Apran Kondwi	**Road Test Instructions**
Vire agòch.	**21** Turn left.
Vire adwat.	**22** Turn right.
Al dwat.	**23** Go straight.
Pakin paralèl.	**24** Parallel park.
Fè yon vire an twa pwen.	**25** Make a 3-point turn.
Sèvi ak siyal men.	**26** Use hand signals.

[1–16]

A. Careful! That sign says "**stop**"!
B. Oh. Thanks.

[17–20]

A. Which way should I go?
B. Go **north**.

[21–26]

A. Turn **right**.
B. Turn **right**?
A. Yes.

Which of these traffic signs are in your neighborhood? What other traffic signs do you usually see?

Describe any differences between traffic signs in different countries you know.

AYEWOPÒ A

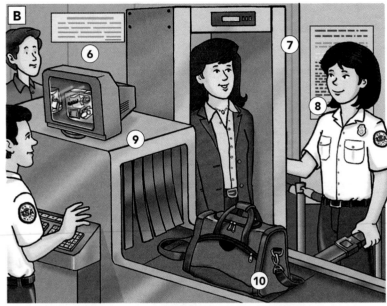

Anrejistreman	**A Check-In**
tikèt	**1** ticket
kontwa tikèt	**2** ticket counter
ajan tikèt	**3** ticket agent
malèt	**4** suitcase
ekran rive ak depa	**5** arrival and departure monitor

Sekirite	**B Security**
estasyon sekirite	**6** security checkpoint
detektè metal	**7** metal detector
ofisye sekirite	**8** security officer
aparèy radyografi	**9** X-ray machine
sakamen	**10** carry-on bag

Pòt depa	**C The Gate**
kontwa anrejistreman	**11** check-in counter
kat pasaj	**12** boarding pass
pòt depa	**13** gate
zòn pasaj	**14** boarding area

Reklamasyon Bagaj	**D Baggage Claim**
zòn reklamasyon bagaj	**15** baggage claim (area)
bagaj	**16** baggage
pòtbagaj	**17** luggage carrier
sak pandri	**18** garment bag
tikèt bagaj	**19** baggage claim check

Ladwann ak Imigrasyon	**E Customs and Immigration**
ladwann	**20** customs
anplwaye ladwann	**21** customs officer
fòm deklarasyon ladwann	**22** customs declaration form
imigrasyon	**23** immigration
anplwaye imigrasyon	**24** immigration officer
paspò	**25** passport
viza	**26** visa

[2, 3, 5–9, 11, 13–15, 20, 21, 23, 24]
A. Excuse me. Where's the _____?*
B. Right over there.

* With 20 and 23, use: Excuse me. Where's _____?

[1, 4, 10, 12, 16–19, 22, 25, 26]
A. Oh, no! I can't find my _____!
B. I'll help you look for it.

Describe an airport you are familiar with. Tell about the check-in area, the security area, the gates, and the baggage claim area.

Tell about a time you went through Customs and Immigration.

PLACES TO GO

PLAS POU ALE

mize	**1**	museum		plas	**11**	park
galri da	**2**	art gallery		plaj	**12**	beach
konsè	**3**	concert		mòn	**13**	mountains
pyès teyat	**4**	play		akwaryòm	**14**	aquarium
plas rekreyasyon	**5**	amusement park		jaden botanik	**15**	botanical gardens
plas istorik	**6**	historic site		planetaryòm	**16**	planetarium
plas nasyonal	**7**	national park		zou	**17**	zoo
mache	**8**	craft fair		sinema	**18**	movies
vann pèpè sou gazon/garaj	**9**	yard sale		kanaval	**19**	carnival
mache	**10**	swap meet / flea market		mache	**20**	fair

A. What do you want to do today?

B. Let's go to { a/an _____ [1–9].
the _____ [10–20].

A. What did you do over the weekend?

B. I went to { a/an _____ [1–9].
the _____ [10–20].

A. What are you going to do on your day off?

B. I'm going to go to { a/an _____ [1–9].
the _____ [10–20].

What are some of your favorite places to go? Where are they? What do you do there?

INDIVIDUAL SPORTS AND RECREATION

ESPÒ AK REKREYASYON ENDIVIDYÈL

ti kous modere/jògin	**1**	jogging	rakètboul	**11**	racquetball
kous apye	**2**	running	pingpong	**12**	table tennis / ping pong
mache	**3**	walking			
wolèbledin/ patinaj egzibisyon	**4**	inline skating / rollerblading	gòf	**13**	golf
monte bisiklèt	**5**	cycling / biking	biya	**14**	billiards / pool
monte planch ak woulèt	**6**	skateboarding	karate	**15**	martial arts
bolin	**7**	bowling	jimnastik	**16**	gymnastics
monte cheval	**8**	horseback riding	leve fè	**17**	weightlifting
tennis	**9**	tennis	egzèsis	**18**	work out / exercise
badmiton	**10**	badminton	bòks	**19**	box
			lit	**20**	wrestle

[1–8]
A. What do you like to do in your free time?
B. I like to go **jogging**.

[9–14]
A. What do you like to do on the weekend?
B. I like to play **tennis**.

[15–17]
A. What do you like to do for exercise?
B. I like to do **martial arts**.

[18–20]
A. Do you exercise regularly?
B. Yes. I **work out** three times a week.

Do you do any of these activities? Which ones?

Which of these activities are popular in your country?

TEAM SPORTS

ESPÒ ANN EKIP

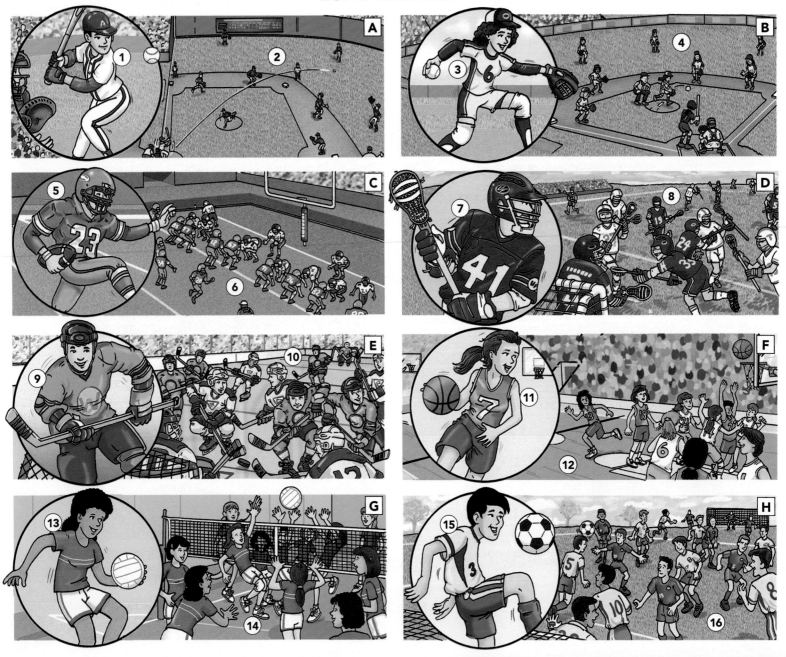

bizbòl	**A**	**baseball**	**hòki/hoki (sou glas)**	**E**	**(ice) hockey**
jwè bizbòl	**1**	baseball player	jwè hòki/hoki	**9**	hockey player
teren bizbòl	**2**	baseball field / ballfield	sal hòki/hoki	**10**	hockey rink
sòfbòl	**B**	**softball**	**baskètbòl**	**F**	**basketball**
jwè sòfbòl	**3**	softball player	jwè baskètbòl	**11**	basketball player
teren	**4**	ballfield	teren baskètbòl	**12**	basketball court
foutbòl Ameriken	**C**	**football**	**volebòl**	**G**	**volleyball**
jwè foutbòl Ameriken	**5**	football player	jwè volebòl	**13**	volleyball player
teren foutbòl Ameriken	**6**	football field	plas pou volebòl	**14**	volleyball court
lakwòs	**D**	**lacrosse**	**foutbòl**	**H**	**soccer**
jwè lakwòs	**7**	lacrosse player	jwè foutbòl	**15**	soccer player
teren lakwòs	**8**	lacrosse field	teren foutbòl	**16**	soccer field

[A–H]
A. Do you like to play **baseball**?
B. Yes. **Baseball** is one of my favorite sports.

A. .... plays __[A–H]__ very well.
B. You're right. I think he's/she's the best _____* on the team.

*Use 1, 3, 5, 7, 9, 11, 13, 15.

A. Now listen, team! Go out on that _____† and play the best game of __[A–H]__ you can!
B. All right, Coach!

† Use 2, 4, 6, 8, 10, 12, 14, 16.

Which sports in this lesson do you like to play? Which do you like to watch?

What are your favorite teams?

Name some famous players of these sports.

ANMIZMAN

pyès teyat	**1** play	mizik djaz	**13** jazz	**pwogram televizyon**	**TV programs**	
konsè	**2** concert	ip òp	**14** hip hop	pwogram jwèt	**20** game show/ quiz show	
klib mizik	**3** music club	**sinema**	**movies/films**	pwogram entèvyou/rakont	**21** talk show	
klib dans	**4** dance club	dram	**15** drama			
klib komedi	**5** comedy club	komedi	**16** comedy	dram	**22** drama	
sinema	**6** movies	katoun	**17** cartoon	komedi/ sitkòm	**23** (situation) comedy/ sitcom	
balè	**7** ballet	fim avanti	**18** action movie/ adventure movie			
opera	**8** opera			pwogram timoun	**24** children's program	
mizik	**music**	fim djab	**19** horror movie	pwogram nouvèl	**25** news program	
mizik klasik	**9** classical music					
mizik popilè	**10** popular music					
mizik konntri	**11** country music					
mizik wòk	**12** rock music					

[1–8]
A. What are you doing this evening?
B. I'm going to { a _____[1–5]____ .
              the ____[6–8]____ .

[9–14]
A. What kind of music do you like?
B. I like **classical music**.

[15–19]
A. What kind of movies do you like?
B. I like **drama**s.

[20–25]
A. What kind of TV programs do you like to watch?
B. I like to watch **talk show**s.

What kinds of entertainment in this lesson do you like?
What kinds of entertainment are popular in your country?

What's your favorite type of music? Who is your favorite singer? musician? musical group?

What kind of movies do you like?
Who are you favorite movie stars?
What are the titles of your favorite movies?

What kind of TV programs do you like? What are your favorite shows?

FÒM IDANTIFIKASYON

1

2

3

4

5

6
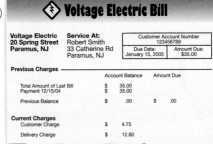

7

8 **WORK PERMIT**

INDIVIDUAL WORK PERMIT:
1. Employer completes and signs
2. Parent or guardian completes and signs
3. Employer submits work permit and LEGIBLE copy of minor's proof of age to the Wage and Hour office.
4. When the approved work permit is returned, the minor may begin work.

GENERAL DUTIES WORK PERMIT:
1. Employer completes and signs
2. Employer submits work permit to Wage and Hour office.
3. The approved duties are returned to the employer. After employer obtains the signature of the minor's parent or guardian then the minor may begin work.
4. Employer must return a copy of the work permit signed by the parent or legal guardian and LEGIBLE copy of proof of age to the Wage and Hour office within seven (7) calendar days of minor beginning work.

☐ INDIVIDUAL WORK PERMIT
☐ GENERAL DUTIES WORK PERMIT APPROVED FOR:
☐ 16 & 17 YEAR OLDS; OR
☐ 14 - 17 YEAR OLDS
☐ APPROVED AS AMENDED
☐ DISAPPROVED

By: _____
Date: _____

Return permit to employer's FAX number:

Section (A) to be completed by EMPLOYER		
Name of Employer:	DBA/	
Employer's Local Mailing Address:	City:	Zip

9 **⚡ Voltage Electric Bill**

Voltage Electric
20 Spring Street
Paramus, NJ

Service At:
Robert Smith
33 Catherine Rd
Paramus, NJ

Customer Account Number	
123456789	
Due Date:	Amount Due:
January 15, 2005	$35.00

Previous Charges

	Account Balance	Amount Due
Total Amount of Last Bill	$ 35.00	
Payment 12/15/04	$ 35.00	
Previous Balance	$ .00	$ .00

Current Charges

Customer Charge	$ 4.75	
Delivery Charge	$ 12.80	

10 **CERTIFICATE OF BIRTH**

(In the Clerks office of the County Commission of Randolf County)

I, MARK PALMER, Clerk of the County Commision in the County and State aforesaid, it being an office of record, and having a seal, do hereby certify that the records in my office show that
_____ Sex _____
Was born at _____ in Bergen County and the State of New Jersey on the _____ day of _____ and that the parents names are as follows:
Father's name _____
Mother's maiden name _____
are recorded in Birth Record No. ____ at page ____ Date filed: _____

In testimony whereof, I have hereunto affixed my signature and official seal at Bergen County, NJ this _____ day of _____ 20 ____.
_____ Clerk

lisans	**1**	driver's license
kat sosyal	**2**	social security card
kat etidyan	**3**	student I.D. card
baj anplwaye	**4**	employee I.D. badge
kat rezidans	**5**	permanent resident card
pas pò	**6**	passport
viza	**7**	visa
pèmi travay	**8**	work permit
prèv rezidans	**9**	proof of residence
batistè	**10**	birth certificate

A. May I see your _____?
B. Yes. Here you are.

A. Oh, no! I can't find my _____!
B. I'll help you look for it.
A. Thanks.

Which forms of identification do you have? When do you need to show them?

U.S. GOVERNMENT

GOUVÈNMAN ETAZINI/AMERIKEN

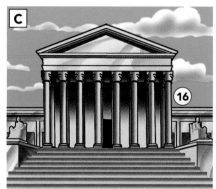

pouvwa lejislatif	**A**	**legislative branch**	vis prezidan	**9**	vice-president
fè lwa yo	**1**	makes the laws	kabinè	**10**	cabinet
depite ak senatè	**2**	representatives / congressmen and congresswomen	Palè Nasyonnal	**11**	White House

pouvwa jidisyè C judicial branch

kay depite yo **3** house of representatives

eksplike lwa yo **12** explains the laws

senatè **4** senators

jij an Kasasyon **13** Supreme Court justices

sena **5** senate

prezidan kasasyon **14** chief justice

Kay depite ak senatè **6** Capitol Building

Kasasyon **15** Supreme Court

Kay Kasasyon **16** Supreme Court Building

pouvwa egzekitiv B executive branch

ranfòse lwa yo **7** enforces the laws

prezidan **8** president

A. Which branch of government [1, 7, 12] ?
B. The [A, B, C] .

A. Who works in the [A, B, C] of the government?
B. The [2, 4, 8–10, 13, 14] .

A. Where do/does the [2, 4, 8–10, 13, 14] work?
B. In the [6, 11, 16] .

A. In which branch of the government is the [3, 5, 10, 15] ?
B. In the [A, B, C] .

Compare the governments of different countries you are familiar with. What are the branches of government? Who works there? What do they do?

Konstitisyon	**A**	**The Constitution**
premye lwa peyi a	**1**	"the supreme law of the land"
Preanbil	**2**	the Preamble

Pwojè Lwa	**B**	**The Bill of Rights**
premye 10 ogmantasyon nan Konstitisyon an	**3**	the first 10 amendments to the Constitution

Premye Ogmantasyon an	**C**	**The 1st Amendment**
libète pawòl	**4**	freedom of speech
libète ekri	**5**	freedom of the press
libète relijyon	**6**	freedom of religion
libète reyinyon	**7**	freedom of assembly

Lòt Ogmantasyon	**D**	**Other Amendments**
fini esklavay	**8**	ended slavery
bay nèg Ameriken dwa pou yo vote	**9**	gave African-Americans the right to vote
etabli enpo sou lajan ou fè	**10**	established income taxes
bay fanm dwa pou yo vote	**11**	gave women the right to vote
bay sitwayen ki gen 18 tan ou plis dwa pou yo vote	**12**	gave citizens eighteen years and older the right to vote

A. What is __[A ,B]__ ?
B. __[1 ,3]__ .

A. Which amendment guarantees people __[4–7]__ ?
B. The 1st Amendment.

A. Which amendment __[8–12]__ ?
B. The _____ Amendment.

A. What did the _____ Amendment do?
B. It __[8–12]__ .

Describe how people in your community exercise their 1st Amendment rights. What are some examples of freedom of speech? the press? religion? assembly?

Do you have an idea for a new amendment? Tell about it and why you think it's important.

HOLIDAYS

JOU FÈT/KONJE

Haitian Creole		English
Joudlan	**1**	New Year's Day
Jou Martin Luther King, Jr.	**2**	Martin Luther King, Jr.* Day
Jou dè Valanten	**3**	Valentine's Day
Jou Memoryal	**4**	Memorial Day
Jou Endepandas/Kat Jiye	**5**	Independence Day/the Fourth of July
Alowin	**6**	Halloween
Jou Veteran	**7**	Veterans Day
Tanksgivin	**8**	Thanksgiving
Nwèl	**9**	Christmas
Ramadan	**10**	Ramadan
Kwannza	**11**	Kwanzaa
Anouka	**12**	Hanukkah

* Jr. = Junior

A. When is___[1, 3, 5, 6, 7, 9]___?
B. It's on _(date)_ .

A. When is ___[2, 4, 8]___?
B. It's in _(month)_ .

A. When does ___[10–12]___
begin this year?
B. It begins on _(date)_ .

Which of these holidays do you celebrate? How?   What holidays do people celebrate in your country?

ETAZINI AK KANADA

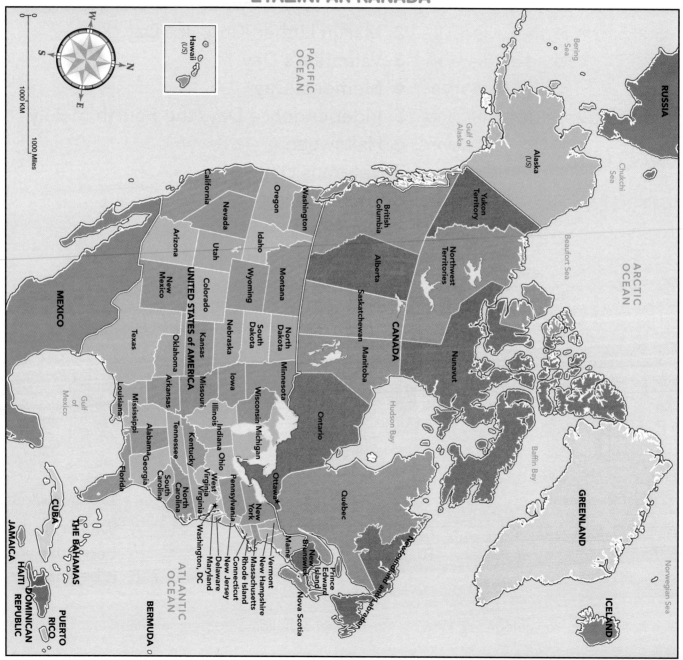

MEKSIK, AMERIK SANTRAL AK KARAYIB

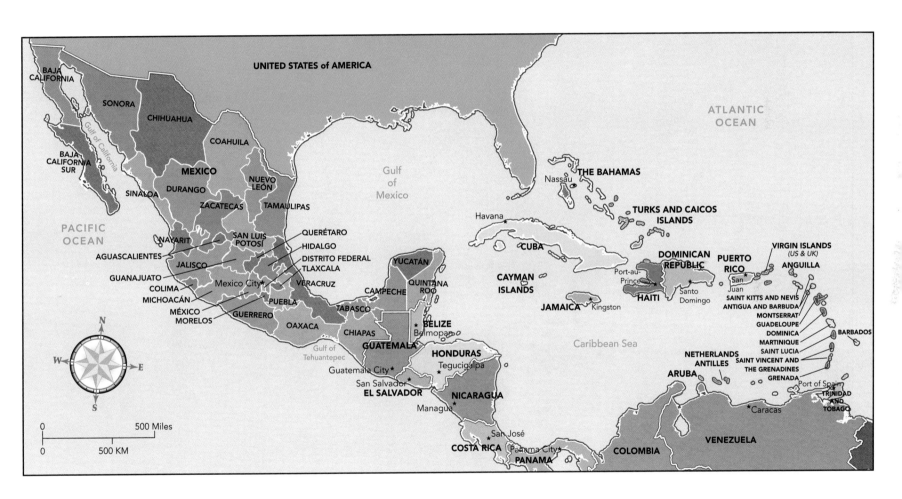

UNITED STATES of AMERICA

BAJA CALIFORNIA

SONORA

CHIHUAHUA

COAHUILA

BAJA CALIFORNIA SUR

SINALOA

MEXICO

DURANGO

NUEVO LEÓN

ZACATECAS

TAMAULIPAS

PACIFIC OCEAN

NAYARIT

SAN LUIS POTOSÍ

QUERÉTARO

HIDALGO

AGUASCALIENTES

JALISCO

DISTRITO FEDERAL

TLAXCALA

GUANAJUATO

COLIMA

Mexico City

VERACRUZ

YUCATÁN

MICHOACÁN

PUEBLA

QUINTANA ROO

MÉXICO

MORELOS

GUERRERO

TABASCO

CAMPECHE

OAXACA

CHIAPAS

BELIZE

Belmopan

GUATEMALA

Gulf of Tehuantepec

Guatemala City

San Salvador

EL SALVADOR

HONDURAS

Tegucigalpa

NICARAGUA

Managua

COSTA RICA

San José

Panama City

PANAMA

Gulf of Mexico

Havana

CUBA

CAYMAN ISLANDS

JAMAICA

Kingston

THE BAHAMAS

Nassau

TURKS AND CAICOS ISLANDS

DOMINICAN REPUBLIC

Port-au-Prince

HAITI

Santo Domingo

PUERTO RICO

San Juan

VIRGIN ISLANDS (US & UK)

ANGUILLA

SAINT KITTS AND NEVIS

ANTIGUA AND BARBUDA

MONTSERRAT

GUADELOUPE

DOMINICA

BARBADOS

MARTINIQUE

SAINT LUCIA

NETHERLANDS ANTILLES

SAINT VINCENT AND THE GRENADINES

ARUBA

GRENADA

Port of Spain

TRINIDAD AND TOBAGO

Caracas

VENEZUELA

COLOMBIA

Caribbean Sea

ATLANTIC OCEAN

N
W E
S

0   500 Miles
0   500 KM

THE WORLD

LEMONN

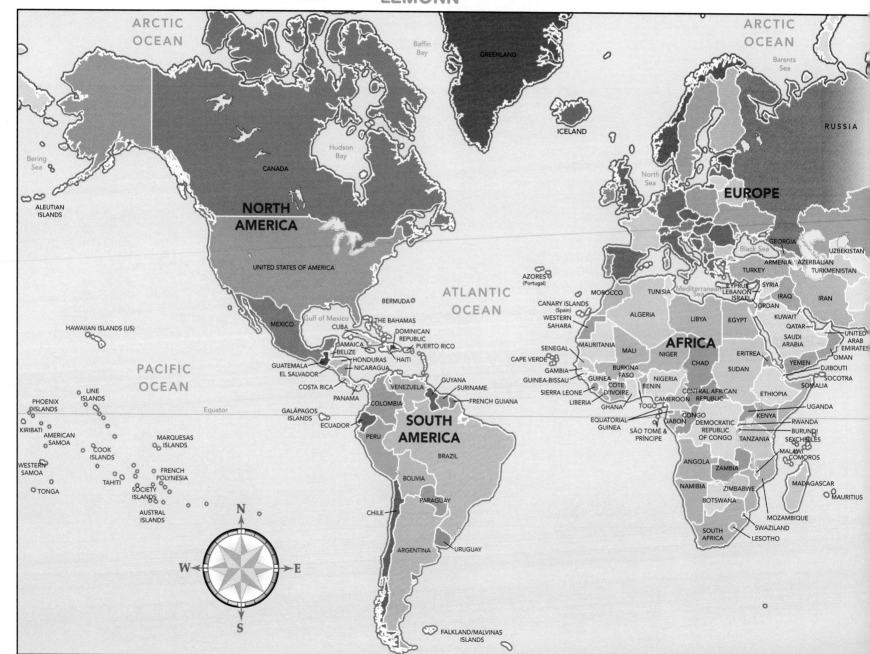

ARCTIC OCEAN

ASIA

Bering Sea

Sea of Okhotsk

KAZAKHSTAN

MONGOLIA

KYRGYZSTAN

TAJIKISTAN

GHANISTAN

CHINA

NORTH KOREA

Sea of Japan

SOUTH KOREA

JAPAN

PACIFIC OCEAN

PAKISTAN

NEPAL

BHUTAN

East China Sea

TAIWAN

DAITO ISLANDS (Japan)

VOLCANO ISLANDS (Japan)

INDIA

MYANMAR

LAOS

PARECE VELA (Japan)

NORTHERN MARIANA ISLANDS

WAKE ISLAND (US)

Arabian Sea

BANGLADESH

THAILAND

VIETNAM

South China Sea

PHILIPPINES

GUAM

MARSHALL ISLANDS

CAMBODIA

YAP

SRI LANKA

MALAYSIA

BRUNEI

PALAU

FEDERATED STATES OF MICRONESIA

SINGAPORE

Equator

NAURU

INDONESIA

PAPUA NEW GUINEA

SOLOMON ISLANDS

TUVALU

INDIAN OCEAN

EAST TIMOR

Coral Sea

VANUATU

FIJI

AUSTRALIA

NEW CALEDONIA

TASMANIA (Australia)

NEW ZEALAND

ATLANTIC OCEAN

FINLAND

NORWAY

SWEDEN

RUSSIA

ESTONIA

North Sea

DENMARK

LATVIA

IRELAND

Baltic Sea

LITHUANIA

UNITED KINGDOM

NETHERLANDS

BELARUS

BELGIUM

GERMANY

POLAND

LUXEMBOURG

CZECH REPUBLIC

UKRAINE

FRANCE

SLOVAKIA

SWITZERLAND

AUSTRIA

HUNGARY

MOLDOVA

SLOVENIA

CROATIA

ROMANIA

PORTUGAL

ANDORRA

BOSNIA and HERZEGOVINA

SERBIA and MONTENEGRO

Black Sea

MONACO

ITALY

BULGARIA

SPAIN

MACEDONIA

ALBANIA

GREECE

TURKEY

Mediterranean Sea

MALTA

CYPRUS

PEYI, NASYONALITE AK LANG

Country	Nationality	Language
Afghanistan	Afghan	Afghan
Argentina	Argentine	Spanish
Australia	Australian	English
Bolivia	Bolivian	Spanish
Brazil	Brazilian	Portuguese
Bulgaria	Bulgarian	Bulgarian
Cambodia	Cambodian	Cambodian
Canada	Canadian	English/ French
Chile	Chilean	Spanish
China	Chinese	Chinese
Colombia	Colombian	Spanish
Costa Rica	Costa Rican	Spanish
Cuba	Cuban	Spanish
(The) Czech Republic	Czech	Czech
Denmark	Danish	Danish
(The) Dominican Republic	Dominican	Spanish
Ecuador	Ecuadorian	Spanish
Egypt	Egyptian	Arabic
El Salvador	Salvadorean	Spanish
England	English	English
Estonia	Estonian	Estonian
Ethiopia	Ethiopian	Amharic

Country	Nationality	Language
Finland	Finnish	Finnish
France	French	French
Germany	German	German
Greece	Greek	Greek
Guatemala	Guatemalan	Spanish
Haiti	Haitian	Haitian Kreyol
Honduras	Honduran	Spanish
Hungary	Hungarian	Hungarian
India	Indian	Hindi
Indonesia	Indonesian	Indonesian
Israel	Israeli	Hebrew
Italy	Italian	Italian
Japan	Japanese	Japanese
Jordan	Jordanian	Arabic
Korea	Korean	Korean
Laos	Laotian	Laotian
Latvia	Latvian	Latvian
Lebanon	Lebanese	Arabic
Lithuania	Lithuanian	Lithuanian
Malaysia	Malaysian	Malay
Mexico	Mexican	Spanish
New Zealand	New Zealander	English
Nicaragua	Nicaraguan	Spanish

Country	Nationality	Language
Norway	Norwegian	Norwegian
Pakistan	Pakistani	Urdu
Panama	Panamanian	Spanish
Peru	Peruvian	Spanish
(The) Philippines	Filipino	Tagalog
Poland	Polish	Polish
Portugal	Portuguese	Portuguese
Puerto Rico	Puerto Rican	Spanish
Romania	Romanian	Romanian
Russia	Russian	Russian
Saudi Arabia	Saudi	Arabic
Slovakia	Slovak	Slovak
Spain	Spanish	Spanish
Sweden	Swedish	Swedish
Switzerland	Swiss	German/French/ Italian
Taiwan	Taiwanese	Chinese
Thailand	Thai	Thai
Turkey	Turkish	Turkish
Ukraine	Ukrainian	Ukrainian
(The) United States	American	English
Venezuela	Venezuelan	Spanish
Vietnam	Vietnamese	Vietnamese

LIS VÈB

Vèb Regilye

Vèb regilye yo gen kat (4) modèl òtograf diferan pou fòm pase ak fòm patisip pase.

1 Ajoute **–ed** nan fen vèb la. Pa egzanp: act → act**ed**

act	burp	deliver	floss	lower	pour	saute	talk
add	cash	discuss	form	mark	print	scratch	turn
answer	check	dress	grill	match	record	seat	twist
ask	clean	drill	guard	mix	relax	select	vacuum
assist	clear	dust	hand (in)	mow	repair	shorten	vomit
bank	collect	edit	help	open	repeat	sign	walk
boil	comb	end	insert	paint	request	simmer	wash
box	construct	enter	iron	pass (out)	respond	spell	watch
brainstorm	cook	establish	leak	peel	rest	sprain	wax
broil	correct	explain	lengthen	plant	return	steam	work
brush	cough	faint	listen	play	roast	swallow	
burn	cross (out)	fix	look	polish	rock		

2 Ajoute **–d** nan yon vèb ki fini an **–e**. Pa egzanp: assemble → assemble**d**

assemble	change	erase	introduce	operate	raise	shave	type
bake	circle	examine	manage	organize	remove	slice	underline
balance	close	exchange	measure	overdose	revise	sneeze	unscramble
barbecue	combine	exercise	microwave	practice	scrape	state	use
bathe	describe	file	move	prepare	serve	supervise	wheeze
bruise	dislocate	gargle	nurse	pronounce	share	translate	wrestle
bubble	enforce	grate					

3 Double konsòn final la epi ajoute **–ed** nan fen vèb la. Pa egzanp: chop → chop**ped**

chop	plan	transfer
mop	stir	

4 Retire **–y** final la epi ajoute **–ied** nan fen vèb la. Pa egzanp: apply → appl**ied**

apply	dry	stir-fry	try
copy	fry	study	

Vèb Iregilye

Vèb sa yo gen fòm tan pase iregilye ak/oswa fòm patisip pase.

be	was	were		leave	left	left
beat	beat	beaten		let	let	let
bleed	bled	bled		make	made	made
break	broke	broken		meet	met	met
bring	brought	brought		pay	paid	paid
build	built	built		put	put	put
buy	bought	bought		read	read	read
choose	chose	chosen		rewrite	rewrote	rewritten
come	came	come		ring	rang	rung
cut	cut	cut		say	said	said
do	did	done		see	saw	seen
draw	drew	drawn		sell	sold	sold
drink	drank	drunk		set	set	set
drive	drove	driven		sit	sat	sat
eat	ate	eaten		sleep	slept	slept
fall	fell	fallen		speak	spoke	spoken
feed	fed	fed		stand	stood	stood
fly	flew	flown		sweep	swept	swept
get	got	gotten		swim	swam	swum
give	gave	given		take	took	taken
go	went	gone		teach	taught	taught
grow	grew	grown		throw	threw	thrown
have	had	had		understand	understood	understood
hold	held	held		withdraw	withdrew	withdrawn
hurt	hurt	hurt		write	wrote	written

VOKABILÈ (KREYÒL AYISYEN)

Nimewo an karaktè gra a endike paj kote mo a parèt. Nimewo ki vin annapre a endike pozisyon mo a nan pòtre a ak nan lis mo ki nan paj la. Pa egzanp, "asyèt **49**-26" endike pozisyon mo *asyat* a se sou paj 49 epi mo a gen nimewo 26.

VOKABILÈ (ANGLE)

The bold number indicates the page(s) on which the word appears. The number that follows indicates the word's location in the illustration and in the word list on the page. For example, "address **3**-5" indicates that the word *address* is on page 3 and is item number 5.

35 millimeter camera **149**-28
A.M. **37**
A.V. crew **191**-12
abdomen **163**-22
above **19**-1
accountant **205**-1
Ace™ bandage **171**-10
acorn squash **99**-13
across the street **227**-7
act **213**-1
action movie **239**-18
activities director **161**-12
actor **205**-2
actress **205**-3
acupuncture **179**-8
acute angle **195**-20a
ad **217**-A
add **117**-10
addition **192**
address **3**-5
adhesive tape **171**-8
adjective **196**-5
adult **85**-7
adventure movie **239**-18
adverb **196**-7
afraid **95**-11
African-American **245**-9
afternoon **43**-5
age **85**
AIDS **173**-25
air conditioner **61**-28
air conditioning **67**-10
air freshener **57**-22
air letter **157**-3
air purifier **179**-11
aisle **111**-1

alarm clock **51**-15
alcohol **177**-10
algebra **193**
allergic reaction **173**-7
aluminum foil **109**-12
ambulance **161**-8
amendment **245**-3,D
American cheese **105**-8
ammonia **69**-14
amusement park **233**-5
anesthesiologist **183**-17
anesthetic **177**-F
angry **95**-1
ankle **165**-11
anniversary **41**-27
annoyed **93**-16
answer the question **13**-19
answer the questions **17**-8
answering machine **149**-26
antacid tablets **181**-8
antibiotic ointment **171**-6
antipasto **127**-10
antipasto plate **127**-10
ants **65**-11c
apartment ads **61**-1
apartment building **45**-1
apartment listings **61**-2
apartment number **3**-8
apex **195**-19a
apostrophe **197**-12
apple **97**-1
apple juice **103**-15
apple pie **127**-25

appliance repairperson **65**-E
application form **217**-F
apply for a loan **153**-F
appointment **41**-28
apricot **97**-7
April **41**-16
aquarium **233**-14
area code **3**-12
arithmetic **192**
arm **163**-25
armchair **47**-29
around the corner **227**-4
arrival and departure board **225**-13
arrival and departure monitor **231**-5
art **189**-19
art gallery **233**-2
arteries **165**-30
artichoke **99**-27
article **196**-4
artist **205**-4
ask a question **13**-17
ask about the benefits **217**-K
ask about the salary **217**-J
ask *you* some questions about your health **175**-E
asparagus **99**-7
aspirin **171**-11, **181**-1
assemble **213**-2
assembler **205**-5
assembly line **219**-4
assist **213**-3
assistant principal **21**-6

asthma **173**-18
athletic supporter **135**-10
atlas **159**-24
ATM **153**-12
ATM card **153**-6
ATM machine **153**-12
attendant **207**-14
audiotape **149**-14, **159**-13
auditorium **21**-K
August **41**-20
aunt **7**-2
autobiography **199**-7
autumn **43**-29
available **217**-6
average height **85**-15
average weight **85**-18
avocado **97**-14

baby **5**-7, **85**-2
baby backpack **55**-29
baby carriage **55**-19
baby carrier **55**-21
baby cereal **109**-15
baby food **109**-16, **187**-1
baby frontpack **55**-28
baby lotion **187**-16
baby monitor **55**-2
baby powder **187**-11
baby products **109**
baby seat **55**-24
baby shampoo **187**-14
baby wipes **187**-10
babysitter **205**-6
back **163**-24
back door **59**-19
back support **223**-7
backache **167**-5
backhoe **221**-18

backpack **139**-24
backyard **59**
bacon **101**-11, **121**-11
bacon, lettuce, and tomato sandwich **121**-24
bad **89**-32
badminton **235**-10
bag **113**-1
bagel **121**-3
baggage **231**-16
baggage claim **231**-D,15
baggage claim area **231**-15
baggage claim check **231**-19
baggage compartment **225**-10
bagger **111**-11
baggy **143**-4
bake **117**-15
baked chicken **127**-14
baked goods **107**
baked potato **127**-18
baker **205**-7
bakery **73**-1
baking products **107**
balance **203**-17
balance the checkbook **155**-16
balcony **61**-21
bald **87**-12
ballet **239**-7
ballfield **237**-2,4
banana **97**-4
band **191**-1
bandage **171**-3

Expressions

NIMEWO, JOU SEMÈN YO, MWA NAN ANNE YO

Cardinal Numbers

1	one
2	two
3	three
4	four
5	five
6	six
7	seven
8	eight
9	nine
10	ten
11	eleven
12	twelve
13	thirteen
14	fourteen
15	fifteen
16	sixteen
17	seventeen
18	eighteen
19	nineteen
20	twenty
21	twenty–one
22	twenty–two
30	thirty
40	forty
50	fifty
60	sixty
70	seventy
80	eighty
90	ninety
100	one hundred
101	one hundred (and) one
102	one hundred (and) two
1,000	one thousand
10,000	ten thousand
100,000	one hundred thousand
1,000,000	one million
1,000,000,000	one billion

Ordinal Numbers

1st	first
2nd	second
3rd	third
4th	fourth
5th	fifth
6th	sixth
7th	seventh
8th	eighth
9th	ninth
10th	tenth
11th	eleventh
12th	twelfth
13th	thirteenth
14th	fourteenth
15th	fifteenth
16th	sixteenth
17th	seventeenth
18th	eighteenth
19th	nineteenth
20th	twentieth
21st	twenty–first
22nd	twenty–second
30th	thirtieth
40th	fortieth
50th	fiftieth
60th	sixtieth
70th	seventieth
80th	eightieth
90th	ninetieth
100th	one hundredth
101st	one hundred (and) first
102nd	one hundred (and) second
1,000th	one thousandth
10,000th	ten thousandth
100,000th	one hundred thousandth
1,000,000th	one millionth
1,000,000,000th	one billionth

Days of the Week

- Sunday
- Monday
- Tuesday
- Wednesday
- Thursday
- Friday
- Saturday

Months of the Year

- January
- February
- March
- April
- May
- June
- July
- August
- September
- October
- November
- December

ENDÈKS TÈM YO

Kreyòl Ayisyen se yon lang endepandan ki ekri jan yo pale li men dapre regleman gramè pa li. Li chita sou vokabilè franse sèzyèm rive dizwityèm syèk epi li sèvi ak regleman gramè lang nan nan peyi Lwès Afrik yo. Li se yon lang nasyonnal tout ayisyen ak pi fò etranje kap viv ann Ayiti pale. Li menm ak franse se de lang ofisyèl peyi a. Ayisyen yo ki fèt oswa kap viv nan peyi etranje pran plezi pale li anpil. Gen ayisyen ki rele lang yo *ayisyen*.

- Òtograf Kreyòl Ayisyen chita sou kat prensip fondalnatal:

  1. Yon siy pou chak son
  2. Menm siy nan pou menm son an
  3. Nanpwen lèt ki bèbè
  4. Chak lèt rete nan wòl li

- Gen dis manman son. Se vwayèl lang nan. Men ki jan yo ekri siy yo:

  a (*papa*), **an** (*manman*),
  e (*bebe*), **è** (*bèbè*), **en** (*benyen*), **i** (*diri*),
  o (*bobo*), **ò** (*bòzò*), **on** (*bonbon*), **ou** (*moumou*).

Sonje: **an en on ou** se vwayèl ak yon sèl son.
  Avèk aksan grav (`) sou **a e o** ou gen **àn èn òn** kòm nan kànva (*kanvas*), pòslèn (*china*), mòn (*hill*).

Son vwayèl yo pa janm chanje.

- **Alfabèt Kreyòl Ayisyen**

aan	b	ch	d	e	è	en	f	g
hi	j	k	l	m	n	o	ò	on
ou	p	r	s	t	ui	v	w	y	z

Sonje: Nan alfabèt kreyòl ayisyen pa gen **u** men **ui**, pa gen **c** men **ch**, pa gen konsòn **q** ak **x**.
Lèt **g** toujou gen son di tankou nan go.
  Pa pwononse lèt **j** kòm si li te gen lèt **d** devan li.
  Pa woule lèt **r** devan vwayèl. Li pa parèt nan fen okenn

Haitian Kreyol is an autonomous and phonetic spelling language based on 16th to 18th century lexical French and syntax principles of West African languages. It is the national language spoken by the entire population of Haiti and by most foreigners living in that country. One of the two official languages of Haiti, with French, it is also the congenial language used by people of Haitian descent born or living abroad. It is written the way it is pronounced, but it has its own grammatical rules. Some Haitians called their language *ayisyen*.

- Haitian Kreyol orthography has four fundamental principles:

  1. One sign for each sound
  2. The same sign for the same sound
  3. No silent letters
  4. Each letter has its own function

- It has ten basic sounds and they are the vowels:

  a (*father*), **an** (*manman*),
  e (*say*), **è** (*get*), **en** (*lens*), **i** (*sea*),
  o (*low*), **ò** (*ought*), **on** (*don't*), **ou** (two).

Note: **an en on ou** always function as single vowels with one sound each. The grave accent (`) modifies the sound of **a e o** which become:
  à as in kànva, **è** as in pòslèn, **ò** as in mòn.

The vowel sounds never change.

- **Haitian Kreyol Alphabet**

aan	b	ch	d	e	è	en	f	g
hi	j	k	l	m	n	o	ò	on
ou	p	r	s	t	ui	v	w	y	z

Note: In the Haitian Kreyol alphabet there is no **u** but **ui**, no **c** but **ch**, and no consonants **q** and **x**. The letter **g** is always pronounced like the **g** in *go*. The letter **j** is pronounced

silab. Se **w** ki ranplase **r** devan **o ò on ou**: wo (*high*), wòb (*dress*), won (*round*), wou (*hoe*). Lèt s toujou pwononse **ès**, li pa janmen sèvi pou **z**.

- Gen senk pwonon: **mwen ou li nou yo**
  Yo toujou apre non ak vèb sòf lè yo se sijè.

- Gen senk atik defini sengilye: **la lan nan a an**
  Yo sèvi selon jan mo ki devan yo fini. Sèl atik defini pliryèl se **yo**.

Menm mo a ka non ak vèb oswa non ak akjektif.

Word by Word respekte òtograf ofisyèl kreyòl ayisyen an ki tabli depi 31 janvye 1980.

Woje E. Saven

like the **j** in *Jan*. Do not roll the letter **r**. It does not occur at the end of any syllable. It is replaced by **w** before **o ò on ou**: wo (*high*), wòb (*dress*), won (*round*), wou (*hoe*). Letter **s** is always **ess**, it never substitutes for **z**.

- The five pronouns: **mwen ou li nou yo** always come after nouns and verbs except when they are subjects.

- The five singular definite articles: **la lan nan a an**, are used according to the ending of the word which precedes them. The only plural definite is **yo**.

The same word is often noun, verb, or adjective.

Word by Word conforms to the Haitian Kreyol spelling, established since January 31, 1980.

Roger E. Savain